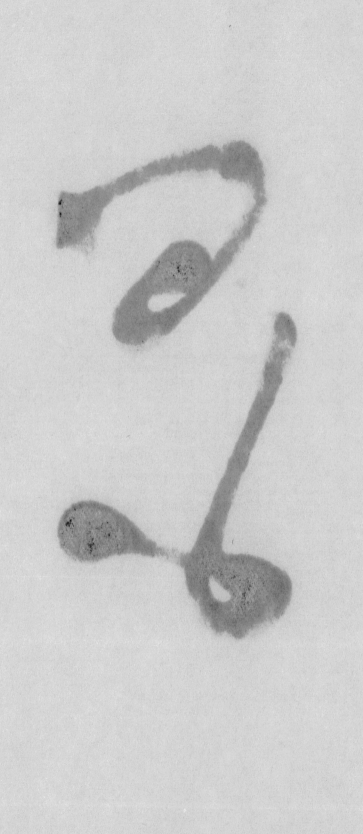

The World of Rotary

The World of
ROTARY

Published by
Rotary International
Evanston · Illinois · USA

Library of Congress Catalog Card Number: 74-18334
ISBN 0-915062-00-3

The World of Rotary (Rotary International publication No. 88)
is available in five language editions—English, French, Japanese,
Portuguese and Spanish—and may be ordered directly from the publisher:
Rotary International, 1600 Ridge Avenue, Evanston, Illinois, U.S.A. 60201.

Editor: Elliott McCleary

Design Consultant: Lawrence Levy

88—(175)—33M

Cover: Nowhere is the internationality of Rotary more
evident than in its annual convention. This scene is a view
of the Rotary International convention in Lausanne,
Switzerland. More than 17,000 Rotarians and their families
from 103 countries attended the five-day meeting.

Foreword

From Argentina to Zambia, a familiar cogwheel emblem announces to those entering thousands of towns and villages and cities that Rotary meets here, that it is at work in efforts to improve the community, help its youth, and reach out a friendly hand to peoples of other lands.

What is Rotary? What is its appeal to men of different nationalities, cultures, and occupations? This book attempts to answer these questions, in photographs and in words contributed by Rotarians and others from scores of nations where Rotary thrives. The result is a kaleidoscopic view of Rotary club activities, and from its astonishing diversity there emerges a global pattern of service.

Rotary was born in 1905. As it marks its 70th anniversary, Rotary clubs have taken root in more than 16,000 communities of 151 lands. Their 760,000 members enjoy a bond of fellowship based upon service to others, a common purpose that relates these business and professional men not only to the lives of their own communities but to the family of mankind.

In publishing this book, Rotary International endeavors to acquaint the Rotarian himself with the wonderful diversity of his own organization and to broaden his concept of Rotary's purpose and opportunities. The book may also serve to inform others in the community about Rotary, friends whose support enables Rotarians to carry out more effectively their motto of "Service Above Self."

Contents

The World of Rotary

What is Rotary?

What is Rotary?

I have concluded that there are more than 750,000 answers to that question. Living answers all over the globe. With due allowance made for structure and organization and connective tissues, Rotary is people—persons imbued with a contagion of spirit that leads to constructive action and makes goodwill a habit.

A French manufacturer works far into the night with fellow Rotarians to arrange a series of career conferences so that 880 graduating boys and girls of his community may get a firsthand view of businesses, professions, and the arts before choosing their vocations. He is ironing out the details for these conferences in nine different kinds of establishments, displaying forty kinds of careers.

"Uncle" Dave Marks, an amateur radio operator, flies 5,000 miles from New York to Bolivia to cut government red tape and permit the emigration of a child of American parents, who are former citizens of Bolivia. Rotarian Marks is used to handling trouble; by means of shortwave radio he marshals immediate help for disasters large and small, as Peruvians and Nicaraguans know from his work right after earthquakes in their countries.

At the Port Elizabeth Rotary Club in South Africa you find members working with teachers from native schools to make exercise books for pupils who have none. In Pusan, Korea, a member arranges for the translation and publication of Rotary literature that will help Rotarians meet community problems. At Alafua in Western Samoa a retired builder

Opposite page: Spokes of a wheelchair outline a Canadian Rotarian and two youngsters enjoying a camp of the Ontario Society for Crippled Children. Such societies trace back to one founded by U.S.A. Rotarians in the early 1920s.

11

from New Zealand works five months with students at a pioneer agricultural college to build an elaborate new facility for pigs.

Pigs and people. Everything goes together in Rotary and in its incredible variety of altruistic activities worldwide. A village in Italy, grateful to a club for its aid in Alpine rescues, renames its main street "Rotary." In British Columbia another kind of rescue takes place when a woman sets out to plant a mile of flowers along Main Street to mark the centennial of the town of Courtnay. When she finds that she will not be able to complete the task in time, she calls on Rotary, and Rotarians take over willingly, assisted by wives and children and other volunteers. In time 9,000 plants display their color along both sides of Main Street.

In none of these cases do Rotarians have anything to gain but the satisfaction of a necessary job well done. The tasks Rotarians undertake are primarily for the benefit of persons outside the pale of Rotary fellowship. What could be the motive?

I began to ask myself that question four decades ago, when activities were a fraction of what they now are. I set out to study the phenomenon of American volunteer groups. I early perceived that service clubs were among the most effective of these groups. And I decided that Rotary would repay inspection not only as the original service club but also because of the successful way in which it caught and expressed the adult and unprecedented view that business was something more than business. I wrote, "Rotary was founded in 1905 by a lawyer who was lonesome in Chicago and no one anywhere has been lonesome since."

No generalization is wholly true, and I grant that in the exuberance of youth I overstated the matter. But I did grasp that the effort of Paul Harris to establish in the complex urban life of Chicago some of the friendliness he had known in Wallingford, Vermont, introduced a new sentiment into the American scene. My interest in the manifestation of this sentiment through the luncheon clubs has not abated during the years, which has led to my role in these opening pages as an interpreter of Rotary to the rest of us.

One feature that seems to me of the highest importance in the workings of Rotary is the autonomy, the selfhood, the integrity of the individual club. For all the far-flung internationality that has evolved, the real unit remains the club, whether it be in Barstow or Bangkok. A direct tie between each member and a local club is basic. There are various ways in which this postulate is stressed. A member cannot transfer. If he leaves town he leaves Rotary. He may be duly elected to become a member of a club in the city to which he has moved, if the classification of the business or profession to which he belongs is open, but, if so, he starts all over again.

The centrality of the club up to now has had much to do with the acceptance and advancement of the original Paul Harris idea. The aim was a fellowship of businessmen that would transcend trade, a fellowship of persons of diverse interests brought together on common ground. A member of the Chicago club travelled to California on business and took the tested idea with him, interesting a San Francisco attorney in founding a club along the lines Harris had drawn. Two other clubs in California and one in Seattle, Washington, followed in short order. New York was next, then Boston. Five years after the formation of the first club, there were sixteen, and representatives from the lot met in Chicago and set up an association. In 1910 a club was established in Winnipeg, Canada. In 1911 clubs were formed in London, Dublin, and Belfast, after which, in 1912, the word "international" was joined with the word "Rotary." Growth continued through the multiplication of local units, and it continues in our time at the rate of more than one new club every day!

Some factor other than the ordinary has to propel such continued growth. From the beginning, almost without plan, there developed a marvelous duality by which men could work in a local club but also in a larger setting that stirred the imagination, that related the local to the general, that gave a feeling of blood relationship discovered through ethical purposes.

Naturally, then, the individual club remained at the heart and center, and it was natural, too, that the constitutional practices ruling the early clubs, having been found good, should become fixed. The classification system can be cited as a further case in point; one man from each vocation or profession is still the basis of Rotary club membership.

Out of this guaranteed diversity, which Rotary deems so vital that it chooses and invites members instead of permitting applications, arises much of the fellowship that draws and holds men. Diversity also encourages a hospitality of mind toward opinions at first sharply at variance with one's own. One Rotarian noted that many Rotarians who have held bigoted views about other countries have had these views changed through attendance at conventions as well as through contact with Rotary-sponsored overseas students.

Emphasis on the club and its multifarious affairs leads to making the weekly meeting and attendance upon it a ritual. Four consecutive absences and you're out, unless you have visited a club other than your own; average Rotary attendance at a given meeting is more than 80 percent of all members.

As a veteran of all kinds of meetings and as one who knows how much of life is lunch, I have become an admirer of Rotary and of bodies that have emulated its meeting techniques. I have enjoyed tracing the influence of the Rotary club on all sorts of gatherings. To begin with, the meetings start on time; more important, they end on time and at an hour you can count on and can schedule your afternoon around. Speeches are short, pointedly so, and I can believe the story that one speaker was given a cake of ice and told he could speak as long as he could hold it.

In some clubs there is at least one rollicking song sung by all, which is a joy in itself and puts the audience in a harmonious mood that helps the speaker. Salutation by first name is encouraged in most clubs, but, whether it is or not, badges with plainly printed names are on every chest. This is one of the practices taken over by many other-than-Rotary clubs.

It would be impossible, although I wish it were not, to calculate the correlation between the act of having a hundred men put their feet under the table together and the results in fellowship and increased insight. We are dealing here with intangibles that can be only savored and not proved. But we do know that something takes place when men (often of the most aggressive type, as one Rotarian points out) break bread ceremonially. The luncheon or dinner (or in a few clubs, the breakfast) is an essential ingredient of the weekly Rotary gathering.

I have spoken before various Rotary clubs. The luncheon I remember best was at Cardiff, Wales, in 1946. All during the grim days of the war the Rotary Club of Cardiff had met at the Angel Hotel. Under austerity, members brought their lunches in brown paper bags. The hotel provided only the tables and coffee. They were still on war rations when I visited the place. But the men came and they ate together and they talked. Then they let the speaker talk. There was plenty of time for the program because no time was spent on serving and clearing. I thought it a real tribute to the Paul Harris idea that men of varying fields should assemble weekly, and, without trappings, enjoy the fellowship of food and keep alive their ideals in the midst of war.

Later I thought back on that meeting when I visited Liverpool Cathedral while it was still under construction. The guard who showed me around explained that the British had kept a token force at work on the job all during the war. "We just did it," he said with more than a touch of pride and insight, "to show Hitler we could build a cathedral while we fought a war." It was, I think, something of this spirit that kept clubs meeting and building during days of destruction.

The meeting at Cardiff also taught me much about the interstitial connection between the local club and the world complex of Rotary—much that has been confirmed by the reams of material I have read since. I found a club with its own peculiar traditions and habits, firmly Welsh, yet not dwelling in isolation or apart. Rather, it was made up of men of reach and outreach, hospitable and responsive to a messenger from afar. I think of Cardiff now as one of more than 16,000 local units wired for sound, each receptive and all sensitively joined by the ganglia of Rotary International.

It is this loose but nonetheless intimate relationship of the clubs that seems to me to make up the genius of Rotary and of the service club idea. The system that administers world service has evolved out of circumstances. It was not foreseen by Paul Harris and it could not have been imposed. It resulted from accommodation and adjustment.

The name "Rotary" was adopted because in the early days meetings were held in rotation at the offices and stores of the members. The emblem is the wheel and it denotes rotation. It's a cogwheel and officially is not given any symbolic significance. But it does stand for mobility. The wheel does represent one of man's first technological devices and it bespeaks the movement of men and ideas from place to place in rapid order. Whether consciously influenced by the symbol of this wheel or not, Rotary International has put the means of rapid communication to the fullest possible use. A secretariat solicits, studies, and distributes comments and data from all over the world, keeping clubs and districts informed on matters of common interest.

One result is the World Community Service Project Library, a compilation in which, in 1974, hundreds of projects (in seventy countries) needing assistance are described and the help of any club anywhere is invited.

Reports of what communities are doing, with or without assistance from other clubs, keep Rotarians alert and geared for action. Activities in one locale may be seen to be applicable to the problems of another. The Rotary Club of Gifu South, Japan, has an anti-pollution committee, for instance, and it also has a great dramatic sense. It has erected signs along the Arata River, enjoining all who pass: "Don't throw rubbish into the river; it is alive and looking at you."

Through good reporting and clear thinking a body of leaflet literature of impressive proportions has grown up around Rotary. It is said that the Greeks had a word for it and Rotary has a pamphlet for it.

A monthly magazine, *The Rotarian* (with a Spanish edition called *Revista Rotaria*) carries news of Rotary worldwide, in cogent text illustrated by action pictures. But it does vastly more. It often displays comment critical of Rotary, aimed at ever higher standards and the improvement of various phases of club life. It also carries articles of general and vital interest, to bring the current world into the meeting place.

In addition, virtually every Rotary club has a weekly publication to keep members well informed. And large areas of the Rotary world are served by attractive, literate, artful Rotary regional magazines printed in seventeen languages including Arabic, Dutch, Japanese, Chinese, French, and Italian.

If a good measure of concern for a cause is the willingness to support it financially, you can get an idea of the feeling Rotarians have for international work by looking over the ledger of The Rotary Foundation. It is sustained by contributions from clubs and indi-vidual members. Donations at this writing were running at the rate of more than five million dollars a year and they were mounting annually. Most of the money goes to an educational program which enables young persons in each of some 350 districts of Rotary International to study in, and have the cultural advantages of, a country other than their own. While abroad, they are befriended and advised by Rotarians of the host country.

In a recent year, more than 800 young men and women received grants for such study and residence, all expenses paid, and these were but the latest of more than 6,400 who have profited by the program in its first twenty-seven years.

Thus Rotary extends itself and its purpose, all of its activities growing out of the service movement which it launched. It is not alone but it is highly representative—singular if not unique. The service club as an institution has become a feature of the civic landscape; it is no longer possible to think either of stability or constructive change without reference to it. As I wrote two decades ago at the time of the 50th anniversary of Rotary, the proliferation of comparable clubs was a most eloquent tribute to the idea of which Rotary has become only a part. The idea anticipated and helped to prepare the way for a day when men would be drawn together into oneness. For all of our failures, thinking is in the direction of wholeness. This is the trend, and, as Sir Norman Angell of England used to say, a trend is more important than a fact because a trend indicates change.

There are trends within Rotary, too, and they may offer some guidance to those who would essay to guess the future. One is attentiveness to youth as a new source of power. Vigorous efforts are being made to expose the young to the concepts of service, and from these efforts many a Rotary club benefits and is renewed. Students in the four school years just before the university level are grouped to form an organization known as Interact. There are more than 3,200 Interact clubs in some seventy countries. Another body is called Rotaract and comprises young men and women between eighteen and twenty-eight who live, work, or study within the limits of the sponsoring Rotary club. Rotaract is now in sixty countries and has an impressive roster of more than 1,900 clubs.

In both Interact and Rotaract women are included, and with their admission comes a further extension of the principle of oneness. For many decades wives have contributed abundantly to the purposes and programs of the clubs. One Rotarian writes with feeling on how women have enriched Rotary. He notes that his wife is active in a women's organization and he is allowed to have no part in the activities of that organization. But she has been allowed to work with him in Rotary projects and he has learned what he and his wife can do by working TOGETHER. (The capitals are his; they put his admiration in lights.)

Obviously, it would take a book to give more than a hint of the variety of Rotary. Fortunately, that book follows. I have sought merely to raise the curtain on it. The reader will find in it a great deal to stimulate further interest. I can only hope that this interest will be as continuous as that which my acquaintance with some Rotarians and Rotary clubs has stirred in me.   —*Charles W. Ferguson*

A world of service

A Rotary club is a group of business and professional men of widely varying occupations who meet weekly, usually for a meal, after which they hear a speaker or discuss affairs related to Rotary's purpose. The aim of their fellowship is to improve their community, work for higher ethical standards in businesses and professions, and promote better understanding among peoples of different nations. As these and other photo pages show, they pursue these goals in an immense variety of ways. Rotary clubs, because of the scope of their membership, are especially attuned to the nature and needs and promise of their own communities and the businesses and professions that they individually represent. Each club tries to analyze the unique problems or opportunities of its area and deal with them in an especially appropriate way, employing the unique capabilities of its members. Thus every Rotary club has a somewhat different agenda and program.

Rotarians of Kaseda, Japan, present gifts to residents of a home for the elderly on the occasion of their nation's Respect for the Aged Day.

The first of 4,000 trees to be planted by the six Rotary clubs of Cyprus is dedicated . . . After storms had devastated one of the Netherlands' few forests, this ax-wielder and fellow Rotarians of Utrecht cleaned out fallen debris and replanted . . . An outrigger boat to be used for commercial fishing by cured lepers is launched with the help of Rotarians of Mandaue, Philippines, who financed it . . . On New Zealand's North Island (opposite page), Rotarians of Rotorua West build a climbing structure for a kindergarten play area.

Angela Teresa Pagani de Nini, a Rotary Foundation Teacher Awardee from Córdoba, Argentina, works with deaf children at Lexington School for the Deaf, Jackson Heights, New York, U.S.A. . . . In Zapopan, México, children play in the yard of a kindergarten and day-care center started by Guadalajara Rotary clubs.

Boys on a Rotary outing in the African bush learn about falconry from an expert. During the one-week camp sponsored by the Rotary Club of Gatooma, Rhodesia, 100 boys ages 8 to 15 are taught everything from fishing and shooting to geology and bush survival.

Rotary-sponsored international exchange students (top) in Australia meet a native emu. Rotary clubs exchange some 6,000 youths annually . . . Refugees in camp near Calcutta, India, receive medical treatment beside ambulance donated by overseas Rotary clubs . . . With closed-circuit TV (opposite page) a child in an Australian school for the deaf can see the movement of her mouth and hear her voice through headphones as she learns to say "kookaburra." Rotarians of Ashfield, Australia, donated the video camera.

Unity in diversity

The typical Rotarian is likely to think of Rotary in terms of his business and professional friends, its focal point as the weekly club meeting, and its boundaries as the city limits of his own town. Rotary, of course, belongs to *his* country. Rotary, however, is truly *international*—a fact that may not be appreciated until a Rotarian attends Rotary's annual convention. There, he mingles with Rotarians and their families from more than one hundred lands, dressed in western clothes, in Indian turbans, in the *barong tagalogs* of the Philippines, in the colorful *dashikis* of West Africa. He may find himself in a gathering of men who appear to be from "back home," yet no one is speaking his language. If there is a twinge of culture shock it is quickly overcome by a growing feeling of kinship, a feeling of being a part of a world family. Eventually the Rotarian realizes that the structure and far-flung reach of his organization have helped him widen his horizons to a world unobstructed by political or social boundaries. The following pages of this chapter provide glimpses of Rotary in various regions of the world through the eyes of Rotarians who live there. Each provides a personal interpretation, not a comprehensive report. Together they convey the flavor and diversity and unity of Rotary as it is lived by some 750,000 Rotarians in more than 16,000 Rotary clubs around the globe.

Opposite page: The annual international assembly, a school for incoming leaders of Rotary's approximately 360 districts, brings people from fifty lands for a week of intensive study and discussion to prepare district governors for their year of voluntary leadership. Simultaneous interpretation in four languages overcomes language barriers. A special day for the wearing of native dress gives photographers a chance to capture the international flavor of the meeting.

Teamwork builds an airstrip for a mission near Kitwe, Zambia, with guidance from the local Rotary club and funds from Rotarians of England . . . Sturdy toddlers show evidence of the good care provided by mission sisters.

Rotary in Africa South of the Sahara

Nearly two decades ago I was privileged to be the governor of what must have been one of the largest districts in the Rotary world. It was the old 25th which covered southern Africa from the Indian Ocean to the Atlantic and stretched from the gold fields of Johannesburg in the south up to Kampala on the equator in the north. Kenya was recovering from the throes of the Mau-Mau emergency; the peoples of Tanganyika, Zanzibar, and Uganda were proclaiming the idea of "Africa for the Africans"; the Rhodesians were endeavoring to find a middle course between this concept and that of white domination; while in the Republic of South Africa the government was feeling its way through the implications of its system of separate development for its multicolored complexity of peoples.

Three years later, I had the good fortune to be sent as the Rotary counselor to visit the non-districted clubs in equatorial and west Africa and spent a month traveling over territory that stretched from Elisabethville in the former Belgian Congo to Fort Lamy in Chad and from Bangui, Central African Republic to Dakar, Senegal. In this vast area I found that some of the erstwhile French colonies had already gained their independence and that the people of Ghana stood on the threshold of receiving theirs. Everywhere I went I was struck by the rising tide of African nationalism and by the feverish march of events.

I was to have followed my tour through equatorial and west Africa with visits to the clubs in Ethiopia and Aden, but was denied this privilege by the aftermath of treatment for malaria, and the opportunity unfortunately did not come my way again. But I do believe that human relationships followed the same perplexing patterns, and political situations revealed much the same delicate problems in these parts, as in the rest of Africa south of the Sahara. As can readily be imagined, human emotions everywhere were apt to run high, relationships between people of different shades of color, culture, and belief to become frayed, suspicions to be easily aroused, and new tensions to develop as crisis followed crisis. And memories of the cruelty and exploitation which marked the old slave days still lingered and rankled.

There were other factors that served to make the picture of Africa even more complicated and difficult. There were many distinct African peoples, each with their own language, code of behavior and pride of nationhood who up to quite recent years had not enjoyed the benefits of any kind of formal education. No African language south of the Sahara had been reduced to writing until after the arrival of missionaries in the nineteenth century—except in the immediate spheres of influence of the Arabic and Amharic writers, and of the Portuguese explorers and traders in places where they had penetrated. Today, large numbers of these millions still suffer from dire poverty and complete illiteracy; they still live very close to nature and follow customs and beliefs that are entirely strange to Western minds.

Add to all this the impact which the miracles of modern science and technology are making on these unsophisticated folk, superimposed on the prevailing stresses of political change and internal strife. From this complex picture will emerge some idea of the field of challenge and endeavor that lies ready to the hand of Rotary in Africa.

In the region that makes up the vast expanse of the continent from the Cape of Good Hope to Chad and from Senegal to Tanzania, and then further east to Malagasy, Mauritius, and their sister islands in the Indian Ocean, the number of clubs has grown from 108 in 1958 to nearly 300, and the number of Rotarians has risen in generous proportion; the total is well over 10,000. While keeping pace in these numerical respects with the tremendous transformation that has taken place in Africa, Rotary has taken care to insure that the composition of its clubs continues to be a true reflection of the colorful spectrum of nationalities, occupations, and philosophies of life to be found in the businesses and professions of the communities served by the clubs. The Rotary Clubs of Accra, Ghana, and Dar-es-Salaam, Tanzania, for example, must be two of the most cosmopolitan clubs that exist in the world today. Especially in the new clubs of the new nations of Africa, the rise of indigenous Africans in the businesses and professions has been reflected in the composition of the clubs.

Rotarians of Africa, since the founding of the first Rotary club in Africa (Johannesburg, 1921) have thrown themselves with diligence into the task of serving their communities and the greater world beyond. The material things Rotarians have provided in the shape of clinics, schools, and social centers bear concrete witness to their energy, dedication, and flair for improvisation. At the same time, in matters of the mind, they have striven to engender among their fellowmen an urge to come together, to talk together and to act together so that in due season a spirit of creative unity in Africa's wealth of rich diversity might happily prevail.   —*J. P. Duminy*

Rotary in Asia

It may have been true when Kipling wrote that "East is East, and West is West, and never the twain shall meet. . . ."

It may be true even today. But it is significant that there are more than 100,000 Rotarians in Asia, members of 2,400 clubs of a worldwide organization that helps to bridge the gaps between men and nations, that has no boundaries of race, religion, color or culture.

Rotary girdles the great land mass of the Asian continent, from Japan, which has more than one-half of all Asian Rotary clubs, through vast India, which has an additional one-fourth of Asian clubs, to Iran and Jordan on the West. It covers Korea, Republic of China, Guam, Saipan, Hong Kong, Macao, and embraces the Philippines.

There is not a single free society in Asia where Rotary does not flourish. Thus, there are some 600 Rotary clubs in India, 27 in Pakistan, and 10 in Sri Lanka. Rotary has returned to Indonesia. It is in Brunei, Singapore, Sikkim, Nepal, Afghanistan, and Bahrain.

Five different languages are spoken in the cosmopolitan Rotary clubs of Thailand and Malaysia; twenty-five different nationalities are represented. One Rotary district of Southeast Asia includes clubs situated in seven different countries. Despite differences of race, nationality, culture, and conditions, these Rotarians and their families and friends meet and mingle in warmth and hospitality; their ideals and aspirations are the same. And the name of Rotary is known and respected—in the Palace, the Government House, the Town Hall, the university and factory. Rotary's good works extend to the *kampongs* and the slums, to the homes and hearts of people less fortunate than Rotarians themselves.

In Vietnam, Korea, Khmer Republic, Laos, Burma, and Bangladesh, Rotary has survived despite strife and has been instrumental in relieving distress and making life a little better. Since 1960 no fewer than one-half million people, mostly refugees from the north, have been treated in Saigon's Rotary-sponsored People's Clinic. Thousands of lives have been saved by this project, made possible by the four Rotary clubs of Saigon and by help from Rotarians around the world. Rotarians worldwide poured in money to help supply food and other needs for refugees of the Bangladesh war of independence.

"Phenomenal" is the only way to describe the energy of Rotary in Japan, where for the last quarter century a new Rotary club has sprung up, on the average, once every eight days. Typical Japanese club projects include the making and distribution of swimming-safety signs and pamphlets; the erection of street lights to deter crime; golf lessons for elderly people; a blood donation drive; and the sponsoring of sign-language courses for the deaf.

Under Rotary's world community service program, many people have been helped. In Thailand, with the help of Rotary clubs of Australia, Denmark, England, the U.S.A., and Canada, Thai Rotarians were able to erect hospitals, schools, and irrigation dams in many parts of the country. Tens of thousands of people are benefiting from these joint efforts. A Rotary club in Australia sent a school teacher, a Rotarian, to teach English pronunciation in a Thai school located in a province bordering Laos, Burma, and China.

A Rotary district in Japan "adopted" a small village in the remote northeast of Thailand, where terrorism of insurgents had been causing great concern to the government and especially the villagers. After Thai Rotarians visited the village, they appealed for help, which came from Japan—building materials and equipment to erect a small electric power plant, a school, and a community hall.

Within a year the project was completed. The school was opened, villagers began to operate the power house, and border police restored peace in the area. From a settlement of 600 families where the children never before had the opportunity to attend school, where people had not known what electricity was or what benefits it could bring, came new life, new hope, and new security. They had never before seen a Japanese, let alone the name "Rotary," but today a picture of a Japanese Rotarian who was instrumental in the building project hangs under a huge Rotary emblem in the school and community hall.

Rotarians differ in practically everything in which men can differ; they have, however, the wish in common to be happy in their personal and family lives and in their friendly contacts with the people around them.

In all of Asia, Rotary emerges as a symbol of peace and understanding, at one with the non-violent teachings of such Asian philosophers as Mahatma Ghandi and Guru Nanak, who preached the universal principles of truth, charity, goodness, and the oneness of mankind. Despite its diversity, Rotary in Asia achieves unity in a most practical sense.

—*Bhichai Rattakul*

The author and monks at the Temple of the Emerald Buddha, Bangkok, Thailand.

Schoolchildren of Cochin, India, line up for food during inauguration of a free midday meal program organized by the local Rotary club, while a Rotarian makes a taste test.

A boatload of boys from Sydney, Australia, begins a three-day stay at Little Wobby Beach camp, built largely by the Rotary Club of Sydney and operated by the New South Wales government.

Rotary in Australia, New Zealand and Oceania

In Australia and New Zealand, where the first Rotary clubs were founded soon after World War I, the composition of the clubs and their atmosphere closely resembles that of Rotary in North America. There is a hearty friendliness and a democratic openness about Rotary fellowship "Down Under," and a vigor that manifests itself in Rotary growth and ingenious club projects.

During the postwar immigration boom, for example, the Rotary Club of Newcastle, N.S.W., met the city's first immigrant ship and pioneered a type of personal interest and help that became formalized in Good Neighbor Councils. Recently, Rotary clubs have shipped crateloads of textbooks to a Papua New Guinea teachers college, organized a riverbank cleanup, sponsored immunology research to improve kidney transplants, and built a $7,000 adventure playground for handicapped children. Out of New Zealand came ROTA (Rotary Overseas Travel Award). Originally a district project, the idea inspired the present Rotary International program for Group Study Exchange Teams. Before girls were admitted to Rotary-sponsored Interact clubs, Australian Rotarians backed "Code Clubs" in girls' schools. Rotarians sponsor an organization known as FAIM (Fourth Avenue in Motion) which has sent out work teams to build wharves and schools and health facilities in Indonesia and Papua New Guinea; one 2-year project involved constructing twelve buildings at a teachers college in western Papua, a project valued at $105,000.

It took twenty-five years to establish the first 100 Rotary clubs in Australia, but since then the rate has speeded up. Today every Australian town of at least moderate size has an oasis of Rotary friendship. There are now about 750 clubs in Australia, with nearly 35,000 members—one Rotarian for every 370 Australians.

Because of the vast and sparsely populated areas of Australia, the early district governors had to travel enormous distances in the course of their terms of office. Even today, when the country is divided into numerous districts, it is nothing for a district governor to travel 30,000 or 40,000 miles in his year to visit the scattered clubs.

Distance between clubs is not such a problem in compact New Zealand, which now has almost 200 clubs and nearly 12,000 members. And the increased speed of international travel has brought the entire Australia-New Zealand-South Pacific area far closer to the rest of the world. Travel by sea to Europe, which used to take well over a month, can now be accomplished by air in 24 hours. Business and cultural interchange has increased so that there is now continual contact with Rotarians from all over the world.

Rotary clubs were first established in 1957 in Papua New Guinea, which Australia has controlled under mandate from the United Nations. Rotary club members have been mostly planters, administrators or businessmen. Because of economic conditions, it has been almost impossible to find indigenous Papuans or New Guineans who could afford membership, but there have been a few cases of success. The future of these clubs—eight at this writing, with some 270 members—will depend on the policy of the government now being set up for self rule.

Rotary has been established in Fiji since 1936; there are now, at this writing, seven clubs with some 250 members. For many years under British rule, it attracted great numbers of Indians who became very successful in business. As a result, a fair proportion of the club membership is of Indian descent. A smaller proportion is indigenous Fijians. Membership of the clubs surely helps comradeship between men of different backgrounds and races.

One finds Rotary established fairly recently in several other South Pacific islands, including American Samoa (with its Rotary club at Pago Pago), Western Samoa, the Cook Islands, Norfolk Island, New Caledonia, New Hebrides, Tonga, and French Polynesia. In this area, the British, French, and Americans have established commercial dominions, but the indigenous population remains stable and a reasonable number of them are Rotary members. The thoughtful Rotarian will reflect on the impact of Western civilization on communities which for centuries have lived undisturbed and content with their own cultures. The acceleration of travel, the spread of business interests and the availability of holiday cruises among the Pacific islands have made the whole area much more accessible. There is no better place for a Rotarian to get quick and sound advice on how best to discover the true nature of the islands than in the Rotary clubs now established in the main towns.   —*Harold Hunt*

The author (left) with friends
at a Rotary outing.

Rotary in Ibero-America

A milestone in the history of Rotary was the founding in 1916 of the Rotary Club of Havana, Cuba—the first Rotary club in a non-English-speaking country. As Rotary founder Paul Harris later wrote, this dissipated the myth that "Rotary was solely an Anglo-Saxon idea; that it never could be appreciated or understood by other races," an idea that had been created by the failure of the first attempt to organize a club there.

As a matter of fact, the concept of such a club at that time was almost an Anglo-Saxon preserve. Many of the first clubs in Latin America were "colony Rotary clubs," begun with mostly Anglo-Saxon members—generally temporary residents. But natives soon became the majority in these clubs and, maintaining high membership standards, assembled the most important representatives of different occupations.

New clubs followed and Rotary successively reached Uruguay, Argentina, Mexico, Peru, Brazil, Chile and eventually all of the other countries of Ibero-America. At this writing, twenty-one countries have fewer than ten clubs, and five have one each. But there are more than 2,300 clubs and 70,000 Rotarians, with 6.5 percent in Chile, 10 percent in Mexico, 22 percent in Argentina and 40 percent in Brazil—which is the fourth country in the world in terms of number of Rotary clubs and fifth in number of members.

Although the clubs of Mexico City and Santiago have more than 200 members, Buenos Aires and Rio de Janeiro more than 300, and São Paulo over 400, the average Rotary club in Latin America has only thirty members, the lowest average in the Rotary world. Spread over very diversified territory, they also differ in size, strength, and efficiency. Those concentrated in metropolitan areas such as Buenos Aires or São Paulo (almost thirty clubs in each one), Lima, or Rio gain strength through mutual association; others too small and remote have a difficult time.

From the beginning, Rotary clubs in Latin America have rendered relevant services to their communities—helping the poor, the aged, the handicapped (especially children); constructing and equipping or helping to sustain schools, asylums and hospitals; cooperating for the betterment of public services and the environment. Rotary clubs have succeeded in helping establish welfare organizations; and their highly qualified membership influences the solution of even the most important national problems.

In general, Rotarians in Latin America are not wealthy. Large donations of money for various purposes are not common. But Latin Rotarians are generous; they put their hearts into service. Especially is this true in youth exchange programs, because big families are common and one extra "son" or "daughter" to lodge or feed is not considered a burden.

Visitors in Latin America are most welcome and quickly are made to feel at home. Formal handshakes are replaced by hearty *abraços* and *abrazos.*

Gay and noisy in their recreation, Latins liven international gatherings. I cannot forget the traffic jam caused in Chicago streets during the 1955 Rotary Golden Anniversary convention, after the Latin American dinner, with Mexicans playing their guitars and maracas and singing amidst tolerant traffic officials and patient drivers.

Many Rotary community assistance activities are aided by "Rotary Anns"—wives and daughters of Rotarians. In Brazil, they are organized in autonomous associations which work in close collaboration with Rotary clubs. They also act independently, as in making clothes for the poor and gowns and dressings for hospitals.

Arduous nationalists, Latin Rotarians cultivate their heroes and salute national flags at the beginning of meetings. But they know how to sustain Rotary's pure internationalism. Rotary gatherings between clubs of different countries are frequent, and clubs of many countries join to send relief to areas devastated by natural calamities such as earthquakes and floods.

There is recognition of Rotary's good works by governments and people all over Latin America. Sixteen countries have issued stamps commemorating Rotary-relevant events. And you will find Rotary and Rotarians commemorated in the names of streets, monuments, buildings, schools, libraries and hospitals.

But the most prized appreciation of the merits of Rotary in Latin America was expressed by Paul Harris in his book, *This Rotarian Age,* referring to the contention that Rotary would only work in Anglo-Saxon countries: "Those who have been privileged to become acquainted with the splendid Latin American Rotarians," he wrote, "know how erroneous were [these] conclusions."   —*Alberto Pires Amarante*

Schoolbuilding, in collaboration with state and church, is a widespread activity of Rotarians in South America. Here, where no school existed, Rotarians of Medellín Norte, Colombia, brought in a railroad car to house thirty pupils and teachers.

Rotary in the United States, Canada, Bermuda, and Puerto Rico

"Help others! And help others to help themselves."

This is the essence of Rotary in action, in the land where Rotary originated and in its neighbor states. This is the way Rotarians interpret and act upon Rotary's solid motto, "Service Above Self."

The "USCB" region includes Rotary in all of the United States, all of Canada, Bermuda, and Puerto Rico. With more than a third of a million members in over 6,000 clubs, it is still the most populous region of Rotary. But with the rapid growth of Rotary International around the world, the organization has long since ceased to have a majority of members or clubs in the U.S. or North America. As Rotary neared its 70th anniversary, 45 percent of all Rotarians and 35 percent of all Rotary clubs were in the U.S.

In Rotary's growth, Canada long has played a great part—and steadily increases its effectiveness. In Winnipeg, Canada, in 1910, the first Rotary club outside the United States was founded, making Rotary, for the first time, truly *international.* Puerto Rico and Bermuda likewise have figured significantly in Rotary history.

Because needs differ in different countries, Rotary action is different. But through it all runs a common thread—service, "help to others." Certainly this is true in USCB!

Here is where Paul Harris lived—and Rotary started and grew.

Here the helpful secretariat is located.

Here governors-nominee come to be inspired and taught.

Here the board meets, and here many R.I. committeemen from around the world come together in meaningful endeavor.

Here, too, incidentally, other great service club organizations have arisen—gaining some of their inspiration from the success of Rotary.

Rotary, of course, is mainly Rotarians in Rotary clubs:

—Rotary clubs that emphasize the uplift of fellowship. Many that stress programs and projects. And most that nicely blend both.

—Rotary clubs exclusively featuring outside speakers. Rotary clubs that, to their own great enrichment, occasionally use their own members as principal speakers.

Here there are many Rotary clubs that find simple ways to encourage high ideals in business. That reinforce their members in making vocational decisions which are long-range and *sound*—rather than "short-cut," expedient, and futile:

—Rotary clubs—always with a broad local cross-section of men in many businesses and professions—that enjoy helping young people learn more about various vocations.

—Rotary clubs that help elevate over-all business relationships in a community or region.

38

And Rotary clubs that spearhead and carry through community service projects great and small. Community service projects, in total, by the thousands! Youth projects, community betterment and health projects. A different project in each community—to meet the greatest local need:

—Rotary clubs that have always taken an intelligent, continuing interest in the youth of the community. Others equally concerned about the aged.

—Rotary clubs doing vital community service without seeking any publicity within that community. But, even more important, alert Rotary clubs using modern public relations techniques as a legitimate tool to help them do a better service job, by involving, for good, an aware and cooperative public.

—Rotary clubs that joyously support The Rotary Foundation in its vital, varied and greatly expanding progress toward world understanding.

—Rotary clubs in the developed countries engaged in worthwhile World Community Service Projects with clubs in developing countries around the world. To help raise the standard of living there a little. For just one example, here started an amazingly successful "Wells for India" project.

—Rotary clubs that participate in helpful activities with visiting students from overseas.

—Rotary clubs that encourage their own members, while traveling and visiting Rotary clubs abroad (as they must, to maintain attendance requirements) to find out more first-hand about the local community service projects of Rotary clubs in developing countries. And to bring back to their own club members a clear picture of those needs, so that organized Rotary help can be intelligent, timely, and meaningful.

—Rotary clubs by the thousands whose members realize that Rotary—while doing its great job at home—truly is one of the few organizations in the world that possesses the machinery, the manpower and the *will* to bring about increased international understanding—perhaps the greatest need in the world today.   —*Warren E. Kraft*

The world's original Rotary club, founded in 1905 by Paul Harris and three friends, thrives in Chicago's Loop. Today it has nearly 700 members. At the meeting shown above, the speaker was Neville Kanakaratne (top, center), ambassador to the U.S.A. from Sri Lanka. Enjoying a stay on a peaceful midwestern American farm, Linda Allison, 11 (opposite page, left), is one of 120 children from Belfast, Northern Ireland, hosted for six weeks by 119 U.S.A. families. With the object of getting the children out of their city during the height of summer civil violence and showing them an area where Catholics and Protestants live in peace, the Rotary Club of Hibbing, Minnesota, U.S.A., sponsored the project and raised $50,000 for transportation and expenses.

With fanfare and a parade, the Junior Olympics for the mentally and physically handicapped get underway with the help of Rotarians of Lesigny, France.

Rotary in Continental Europe,
North Africa and the
Eastern Mediterranean

Rotarians of my region of the world are citizens of twenty-nine nations, speak seventeen native languages, are Roman Catholics, Jews, Muslims, Greek Orthodox, and Protestants. Their homelands range from Iceland and the Faroe Islands out in the Atlantic down to Turkey in the east, and from Norway's North Cape far above the Arctic Circle to Egypt in the south.

There are more than 120,000 Rotarians in CENAEM, the Continental European, North African, and Eastern Mediterranean region. They represent a great variety of cultural backgrounds; they function in diversified social structures resulting from varying stages of industrial and social-welfare development.

Contributing to their diversity is the Rotary practice of choosing members from every recognized business and profession in the community—in order that fellowship might develop from differences rather than similarities of interest.

Today it is more difficult than it once was to find a need that can be filled by a club project; in most CENAEM countries, centralized social-welfare institutions meet many former community deficiencies. But new outlets for service have arisen, especially in service to youth. And these new projects are as diverse as human needs are varied.

Accordingly, Rotary clubs support an orphanage in Turkey for earthquake-stricken children. Various Egyptian Rotary clubs work to eliminate illiteracy, and one supports a birth-control information project. A German club provides financial and personal support for activities among juvenile delinquents. A club in The Netherlands transports handicapped children to a swimming pool weekly, and another in Sicily has donated a complex heart-disease detector to school authorities for periodic health checkups of school children. A Swedish club, in my own district, sent a special woodworking machine to a school for handicapped carpenters in India.

International youth exchange is a popular activity of CENAEM Rotary, involving family hospitality, camps, and excursions. A strong network of intercountry committees that developed after World War II coordinates this exchange, together with intercountry visits of Rotarians and their wives.

As European Rotarians travel on business throughout the gigantic, in a true sense revolutionary, slowly progressing, European Common Market, they visit each other's clubs. Many clubs have one or a few visitors from other countries at every meeting.

CENAEM Rotarians have strong personal reasons to promote international friendships, having seen the effects of two world wars in their homelands, and on Rotary itself. On this side of the Atlantic, Rotary was first established in Dublin, Ireland, in 1911, six years after Rotary was founded in Chicago. However, because of World War I, the organization was not firmly grounded on continental soil until ten years thereafter. Rotary between the two world wars expanded to some 500 clubs in twenty-six continental countries and geographical regions. During World War II all were disbanded, save those in Portugal, Switzerland, Finland, and Sweden. These disbanded clubs were re-established after the war, excepting those in ten countries (Czechoslovakia, Hungary, Yugoslavia, Rumania, Poland, Danzig, Latvia, Estonia, Lithuania, and Bulgaria). In 1945 Rotary had to start almost from scratch, and in that year, more than sixty clubs were readmitted. Today there are more Rotary clubs and Rotarians in the region than ever, and growth continues. In Germany there is one Rotarian for every 4,424 inhabitants; in Austria, for every 3,910; in Italy, for each 3,318; and in France, for every 2,456. In Norway and Sweden there is one Rotarian for every 484 inhabitants.

Rotary, in my region, is strong and flourishing. It is important on the national as well as the local level, with a membership that includes national leaders in industry, commerce, politics, science, the humanities, and religion, in addition to a broad representation from local businesses and professions.

Today, wherever you live, you cannot avoid feeling at one with the rest of the world. There is a heightened exchange of scientific discoveries, of commodities and resources, as well as united endeavors in various fields to solve the great problems of humanity—all advanced by communications and the mass media. There is a new imperative for the individual to seize his responsibility as a world citizen.

This approach to a broadened outlook is not new to Rotarians, who have long sought to advance international understanding, goodwill, and peace. For the average Rotarian of my region, thus, tradition incites him to be loyal to that objective and to look on the future as a challenge which he shares through the universal brotherhood of Rotary International with hundreds of thousands of equally service-minded men throughout the world.

—*Ernst G. Breitholtz*

The author in a Roman amphitheatre in southern France.

Rotary in Great Britain and Ireland

Rotary has been part of the British and Irish scenes almost as long as there have been Rotary clubs in any part of the world. The Rotary Club of Dublin, Ireland, dates back to 1911, as do the clubs of London, England, and Belfast, Northern Ireland. There have been Rotarians in Manchester, England, and Glasgow, Scotland, since 1912.

Today, the region known as Great Britain and Ireland (GB&I)—including not only England, Scotland, Wales, Eire and Ulster, but the Channel Islands, the Isles of Scilly, the Isle of Wight, the Isle of Man, the Orkneys and Shetlands—is divided into two dozen districts with some 1,200 clubs and 55,000 members.

What draws so many men to Rotary? What is it that appeals to them? I think that in every instance it is the need for fellowship and the desire to serve—and the enjoyment that there is to be found in working together, in carrying out the ideals and the object of Rotary.

The challenge of service takes a somewhat different form in each club—depending upon such factors as the needs of the local community and members' interests in other countries. Some personal memories may serve to illustrate the width and extent of Rotary service:

Cork, Ireland: Here, 640 Rotarians and their ladies from north and south and west, from both Northern Ireland and the Republic, gather for a district conference. There is unity in fellowship and a determination to continue to work for better and more peaceful days.

East Anglia, England, District 108: A recollection of tireless service and cooperation with other service organizations helping with the Asian refugees from Uganda.

Mendip, Somerset, England, District 110: Memories of cooperation by all the service organizations after the tragic air disaster near Basel, Switzerland, in which almost 100 young housewives and mothers from a group of Somerset villages, on a day's outing, were killed or injured. Many had to be hospitalized in Switzerland.

Scarborough, England, District 104: A gay, cheerful, furnished house with a treatment room and a bright garden a few minutes' walk from the sea, where a man or a woman dependent upon an artificial kidney machine can stay for a week's holiday, with his or her family.

Ambleside, England: The local YMCA center was about to close down for lack of money, but now a group of eager young men and women under the banner of Interact is busily raising funds to save it. The Interact club is sponsored by the Rotary Club of Ambleside. A few years ago Ambleside Rotarians sent drilling rigs to Bihar, India, for the digging of hundreds of urgently needed wells.

Risca, England: Here is the Rotary club which launched "Operation Self-Help," an undertaking between Risca, its fellow clubs, and the Rotary Club of Ranchi, India. The project has brought water, increased crops, a school and health services to a group of Indian villages.

Throughout Great Britain and Ireland, Rotarians are aware of the opportunities presented by 70,000 overseas students (plus nurses) undertaking higher studies here. Rotarians find ways by which many of these young people can be welcomed and made to feel at home during their stays.

Rotarians are involved in youth exchange and in responding to the needs of youth generally. They are similarly active in discovering and answering the needs of the aged and of the mentally and physically handicapped. There is general enthusiasm for group study exchange and a realization that these young business and professional men, sent abroad in small groups on Rotary study tours, may well be holding positions of the utmost responsibility in their own countries in the years to come.

Yes, Rotary throughout Great Britain and Ireland is very alive and active. We are well aware that we have reached the end of an epoch, and that there is need to think afresh about the problems which are likely to be with us until the end of the century.

And why is there this activity? What do we hope to achieve? Perhaps we hope that through fellowship can come service, and that through service can come understanding, and that through understanding can come something even more important: a greater realization that the ideals of Rotary mean much more now in the world of the 1970s and 1980s than ever they meant at the beginning of the century.   —*John Savage*

The author visiting a Rotary-supported overseas book project.

A program to make sure that the elderly are not forgotten is an important activity of Rotarians in Crowborough, England. Similar projects are prevalent throughout Great Britain and Ireland.

What Rotary means to the community

In the life of a town or city, a Rotary club performs a unique role. The club is in fact a sociological phenomenon; it can do things which other human instruments cannot do, or do as well.

An important reason for the effectiveness of a Rotary club is its initial design: members represent virtually every recognized business and professional activity in the community. This cross-section of the community's social, economic, and cultural life can become an ideal forum and information resource in matters concerning vital issues confronting the community. If club members are gifted with intuition and imagination, as often happens, together they can enlighten the community regarding its needs, present problems which need to be solved, and discuss situations which could not be faced conveniently without the help of unselfish persons. In effect, they can act as mediators between the citizens and the political and administrative authorities.

There are limits, of course. Rotary clubs can commit themselves more completely in nations with traditions of greatest freedom, less so in states that have arrogated to themselves all of the more complex and extensive tasks. Rotary clubs frequently have more latitude and influence in small towns as compared with large cities. In smaller centers, the life of the community goes on under everyone's eyes. Problems therefore may be easier to see and comprehend, solutions easier to grasp, and coordination of efforts not such a problem.

Opposite: Down the street of a small Japanese village proceeds a busload of members of the Rotary Club of Gifu South who have come to provide legal and medical services and to present the community with an electronic organ.

Because it is a service club, Rotary cannot be replaced by other types of institutions and organizations. A service club by its nature is concerned with the good of the community, in small matters as well as in large.

In many countries, the activities of Rotary have remained unknown because its members avoid publicity; but recently, we have thought it useful to inform the public of the accomplishments of Rotary in order to give an answer to the frequent questions, "What is Rotary?" and "What does it do?"

Although it is in an ideal position to provide advice to public authorities, a Rotary club does not often do so directly. But many times, through their programs, projects, and debates, Rotary clubs have shown public authorities effective ways to solve community problems. The qualifications of Rotarians, for example, make them highly suitable persons to advise on city development projects and plans for the construction of schools, libraries, museums, hospitals, and rehabilitation centers for juvenile delinquents.

In some states and communities around the globe, Rotary clubs rather than public authorities were the first to examine local ecological problems. Air and water pollution are a serious concern of many Rotary clubs.

Often a Rotary club may be found at work, in the most direct and informal way, in situations where public authorities are not present. It may be adoption of a school or care of the blind in countries where government funds are insufficient, the planting of flowers in town districts blighted by too much traffic, the rehabilitation of young drug addicts or a search to find a remedy for juvenile delinquency. Recently, some Rotary clubs have concerned themselves especially with the psychological needs of the aged—to make them feel they are still useful, to rescue them from the isolation which, near the end of life, can be the cause of serious depression.

Projects for youth have been among the most popular of Rotary projects. For example, a large building to house Italian youths studying in Paris, Maison d'Italie, was sponsored, planned, and partially funded by the Rotary Club of Milan, Italy.

When earthquakes, floods, famines, and other natural disasters occur, Rotarians rush to help the victims. They send money and supplies, and they work to help the unfortunate. I remember, for example, some years ago when many hundreds of refugees from an Eastern European country were housed in a camp near our town. At the end of a meeting of the local Rotary club, the club president asked the members to help these people who, to safeguard their basic rights, had left everything—their homes, their country, their dearest things. Immediately, the Rotarians placed a large amount of money at the president's disposal. The Rotarians' wives went to the tradesmen of the town and bought clothes at half price, took the clothes directly to the refugee camp, and in many cases offered refugees the hospitality of their homes.

This is the spirit of Rotary, which provides to the poor, the unlucky, and the disinherited the attention and the care of those who wish to redeem the wickedness and miseries of life with generous and disinterested actions, in the name of our common human condition. Rotary, moreover, helps its members and others realize that the real value of life does not lie in wealth, but in the capacity of discerning what is essential to the spirit, and what unites men beyond differences of race, religion, and social condition.

Rotary surely will perform a vital role in the communities of the future. The future is likely to be full of menace to man's freedom and well-being. Technological advancement will continue, but it may, as at present, be accompanied by the degradation of moral qualities. Man has landed on the moon. But his moral progress is not so great; this we can realize every day. Let us think for a moment about how easy it is for us to reach distant places and yet how difficult it can be to understand the mood of a person close to us, and to help that person.

Man will not be able to save himself without meditating seriously upon his future. Rotary clubs, through their humanitarian and civil concerns, have done much to make their communities more livable. In the future, they must continue to discover new ways of service and of working together on what is really human and valuable.   —*Tristano Bolelli*

The helpful neighbor

Most Rotarians help their communities as individuals by lending their expertise and support through established agencies, such as those concerned with youth, the handicapped, and the arts. But many clubs also engage in collective efforts, as these photos demonstrate. Because its members are a cross section of the business and professional life of the community, the club is a good forum in which to discuss certain community affairs which would benefit from an exchange of opinion. And it frequently serves as a catalyst in getting needed improvements underway. A Rotary club is not a charitable organization dispensing funds, although some occasionally employ a specific fund-raising effort to accomplish the task. Typically, a Rotary club's function in the community is to find a need, to help alleviate that need through support of an established agency or, if an agency doesn't exist, to get one started. The club then usually hands over to others the task of ongoing support, leaving the club free to continue in its creative role.

When floods destroyed food supplies in Chiengmai, Thailand, Rotarians rushed sacks of rice to the devastated area.

On a green hillside in Guayaquil, Ecuador, is the brightly modern Fasinarm school for some ninety mentally handicapped children ages 5 to 18. Rotary clubs paid for the building; the government provides the teachers . . . Rotarians of Wakayama, Japan, sweep clean an approach of Wakayama Castle. Cleanup and environmental work has been an activity of Rotarians for decades.

"Pedrito" (top), deaf and mute, discovers the world of sound with a hearing aid fitted at the Paul Harris school for special teaching sponsored by the Rotary Club of Mercedes, Argentina . . . A small school for the deaf and mute in Lyallpur, Pakistan, is helped by the local Rotary club . . . Slow learners and the mentally handicapped (opposite page) gain skills and confidence in a rehabilitation institute's carpentry shop equipped by the Rotary Club of Guebwiller, France.

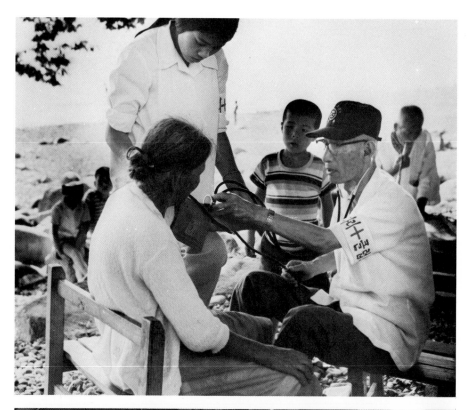

A free clinic (top) to provide physical examinations and medication was sponsored by Rotarians of Namhai, Korea . . . In Burlington, Wisconsin, U.S.A., a town of 8,000, the Rotary club sponsors the community's only rescue squad and the ambulance service. Half of the volunteers are Rotarians . . . Lifesaving equipment (next page) for use on the beaches of Lima, Peru, has been donated by Rotary.

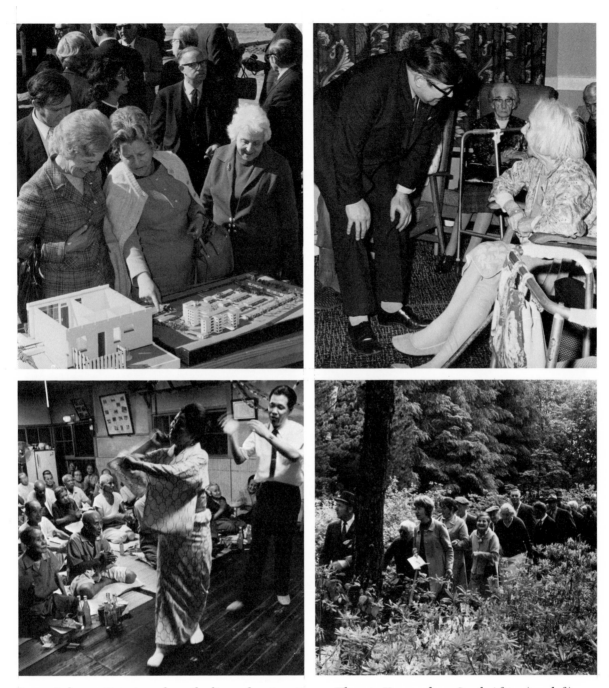

In myriad ways Rotarians cheer the lives of senior citizens. Thus, in Krugersdorp, South Africa (top, left), a Rotary Golden Age Village for the aged is announced . . . A Rotarian of Caerphilly, Wales, shares a warm moment with one of a group of elderly viewing a Rotary-club sponsored movie . . . Rotarians in Wakayama, Japan, sponsor entertainment in a home for the aged . . . Rotarians of Zurich-Knonaueramt, Switzerland, take oldsters on a rhododendron walk . . . Personal coaching (opposite page) and golf clubs were gifts by the Rotary Club of Amagi, Japan, to oldsters living near the course.

Preserving one's heritage is part of community service. In Noshiro, Japan, festival music peculiar to the area, not heard for forty years, is resurrected by the Rotary club, which recruited 70- to 80-year-old musicians who recollected the old tunes and played them into a tape recorder. The club distributed tapes to local schools and a tourist association . . . Each year (opposite page) the three Rotary clubs of Mt. Isa, Australia, evoke the area's frontier past with a world championship-class rodeo.

Fund raising takes many forms. Music (above) from a 208-year-old organ lures donations in St. Austell, England . . . In Sacramento, California, U.S.A. (opposite page, top) an elegant classic auto show garners $5,000 for crippled children . . . And in Porbandar, India (opposite page), Rotarians march and man a poster-decorated truck to campaign for cash, food and clothing for monsoon flood survivors.

Parties with a purpose: Donations of necessities (top left) are collected by "Operation Giving" of the Rotary and Interact Clubs of Bogotá, Colombia, for distribution to poor children . . . An Old English evening sponsored by the Rotary Club of Pietermaritzburg East, South Africa, raises money to build Bantu classrooms . . . "Sewing bees" of Rotarians' wives in Lima, Peru, produced these bundles of clothes for the old and poor . . . Eyes and smiles gleam at a Christmas party staged by the Rotary Club of Brisbane West, Australia, for children whose fathers are far overseas in the armed forces . . . More than 150 mentally handicapped youngsters (opposite page) are guests at an annual Christmas party of the Rotary Club of Arden Arcade in Sacramento, California, U.S.A.

Rotary and the next generation

From the early days of Rotary, most Rotarians have been family men. And so it was natural that their solicitude for their own children soon expanded to embrace others' children, in their own communities and in faraway places of our one world.

Thus, when the 18-year-old son of a Rotarian in Elyria, Ohio, U.S.A., died because of inadequate emergency medical care following a tram accident, the father began work to prevent recurrence of such a tragedy. He sold his business and headed a drive that built a specialized hospital. He became intensely concerned with the plight and the neglect of crippled children and in 1919 persuaded fellow Rotarians to join with him in founding the Ohio Society for Crippled Children. With considerable help from Rotary clubs, that statewide group developed into the national Easter Seal Society of the U.S.A. Today, Edgar F. "Daddy" Allen's dream of care, treatment, and education for the world's handicapped is advanced by a direct descendant of his original society—Rehabilitation International, a federation of organizations serving the disabled in sixty-one countries. In addition, hundreds of Rotary clubs work locally with handicapped children. The Rotary Club of Chicago sponsors an extensive rehabilitation clinic where the youngsters can receive therapy and training in the use of devices to overcome their handicaps. In Taitung, Taiwan, a residence clinic accommodates sixty-five children with varying degrees of handicaps resulting from poliomyelitis. The home is supported by nineteen Rotary clubs—eighteen in the U.S.A., one in Taitung.

Opposite page: Youngsters of Ulverstone, Australia, enjoy a play rocket and slide hand-fabricated by local Rotarians.

67

Rotary has always served the next generation. Rotary clubs sponsor Boy and Girl Scout troops, support YMCAs, boys clubs, youth clubs, summer camps, playgrounds, swimming pools, and parks, provide loans and scholarships to college students and awards to technical trainees, stage career days for students, and conduct essay contests and art fairs to encourage young talents.

Thousands of secondary-school youngsters cross international borders annually to tour or study abroad under Rotary auspices. Over the years, thousands of college students have pursued advanced study abroad thanks to The Rotary Foundation, which has recently expanded the scope of its program to include non-academic activities advancing international understanding.

A new dimension for Rotary came about in 1962 with the founding of Interact, a club for teenage youth. Every Interact club is sponsored by a Rotary club, and engages in projects serving the community and promoting world understanding. The service club has been one of the most venturesome and significant developments in Rotary. Originally, Interact admitted only boys. Today it enrolls both girls and boys, who are recruited from the four years of school preceding university.

From five Interact clubs in 1962, located in Mexico, India, Italy, and the U.S.A., Interact has grown to more than 3,000 clubs in seventy countries with 70,000 members.

The creation of Interact and its quite phenomenal success led inevitably to the founding of another organization five years later. "What happens after Interact," asked its young members, "when we leave school and proceed either to work or to university?" Rotaract was the answer.

Rotaract is an organization of young people aged eighteen to twenty-eight dedicated to the ideal of service to the community, to their vocation, and to mankind. Like Interact clubs, the clubs of Rotaract are each sponsored by a local Rotary club.

In its first five years, Rotaract attracted some 35,000 members in sixty countries, easily spanning differences in nationality, race, religion, and language. Like Interact, it thrives around the world, its popularity not easily attributable to national characteristics or to any other factor—except the incidence of local Rotary interest and enterprise.

All of these activities bring Rotarians and young people together so that a phrase frequently heard these days, in place of "Service to Youth" is "Service *with* Youth." This is especially appropriate for the 1970s and 1980s.

The newer phrase recognizes some of the characteristics of our age—the increasing sensitivity of young people to injustice, to pain, to inhuman values in their world; their anger, their compassion, and their readiness to act, their own vulnerability to maleficent influences and pressures of overwhelming impact; their demand for a voice in planning any new worlds.

Interact and Rotaract provide excellent opportunities for young people and their seniors to talk and plan and work together in mutual respect and friendship. Other such opportunities occur in other contexts. For example, in Australia, winners of Rotary Youth Leadership Awards (RYLA) meet with Rotarian advisers in week-long seminars on leadership.

Interact . . . Rotaract . . . youth leadership award programs . . . together they paint a picture of wide-ranging activity with youth, but they are not the whole picture. For example, the Rotary Club of Vijayawada, India, developed a children's library as part of a children's park. The Rotary Club of Cadiz, Kentucky, U.S.A., led a community drive for a $100,000 library and youth center—and this was in a community of 2,000 people.

In Portugal, Rotarians conduct annually the "Camp of Work and Social Service." At a recent session, twenty-three young people from thirteen countries came together to do social work among the fishermen families of the area. In Umtali, Rhodesia, wives of Rotarians are active in helping their husbands who work on the local "Samaritan House," a home for girls. Thousands of Rotary clubs sponsor scouting units for boys and girls.

The rapidly changing nature of our society is making a tremendous impact upon our youth. Modern technology has freed young people from the need to go to work at an early age and has required them to undertake increasingly sophisticated technical training. Postponement of vocational responsibility, increased personal academic knowledge and maturity, earlier granting of political rights, increasing mobility financed by social prosperity, the loosening of family bonds, the paradox of the widening gap between wealth and poverty, the increasing evidence of the spoliation and destruction of the earth's wealth, the revolt against materialism, the passionate advocacy of many idealistic causes—all have combined to produce a turbulence of ethical and moral standards, an impatience with established authority and a critical reaction against accepted religious and social shibboleths.

In work toward a secure future, Rotary has an increasingly potent part to play—in close partnership with youth. The Rotary practices of friendliness toward all peoples of whatever race or nation or creed, of service to one's neighbor near and far, of training and encouragement of leadership, are fundamental to a nobler destiny for mankind.

Rotary clubs can and do participate in the provision of the tools of education—from books to computers; in the building of places of education—from adventure camps to universities; in the training of youth in the means to serve society through work—from better cultivation of rice paddies to the building of spacecraft. But the most vitally important role for Rotarians in the future is service with youth, dialogue with youth, listening to youth, in engaging the idealism, the energy, the imagination, the enterprise, the courage of youth in the great adventure into the future. To the next generation Rotary must mean companionship and service. To Rotary the next generation means—and always will mean—the future of mankind.   —A. R. (Bert) Dreaver

Inside Interact

During my freshman year of high school, my brothers and friends introduced me to Interact.

Interact, I learned, is a service club for high-school age youth. Members of more than 3,200 Interact clubs in about seventy countries share in a world fellowship dedicated to service and international understanding. Their concern is translated into school, community, and international service projects.

Each club is sponsored by a local Rotary club. Rotarians listen as Interact members develop plans, then offer guidance and friendly encouragement. Two-way exchange between the Rotary and Interact clubs is emphasized and is found to be mutually beneficial.

The individual Interact member soon learns other basics of Interact. The club is often associated with a high school. When it is, guidance is also given by a school advisor, usually a teacher. The club meets semimonthly or weekly, with the time and place varying with each club. Lunch meetings at school are common, but so are dinner meetings involving a program of both club business and a special speaker or entertainment.

The heart of an Interact club is its projects. At my introductory meeting I listened as possible projects were discussed. Some involved raising money: to buy a needed item for school, to provide equipment for the handicapped, to help other community service organizations, or to provide aid to an area hit by disaster. Other projects emphasized direct action with people: painting or repairing school buildings, taking mentally handicapped children to a zoo, collecting for established community services, running a canned-food drive to provide holiday food for the less fortunate, and corresponding with pen pals of other countries.

Interested by the goals, possible projects, and friendly members, I applied for membership in the club and was accepted. New members were welcomed at a special party.

Now that I was a member I was also responsible for developing projects—not an easy task. Projects take thinking, time, and work. They are best when they involve the entire club. Members labor and learn with each other, with advisors, Rotarians, and those they seek to help. The division between helper and helped fades as both benefit from the experience.

Projects sometimes surprise you. What started as a fund-raising spaghetti dinner sponsored jointly by our Interact Club and our school's International Friendship Club burgeoned into an annual event. We served food and provided entertainment for about 400 people—bridging the "generation gap" as parents, members, other students and friends enjoyed it together.

Interact spans the seas in its service. When a former teacher serving in the Peace

At an Interact district convention in Kakuda, Japan, a group of Interactors and their Rotarian advisers meet for discussion in an old bell tower. Interact is a service club for boys and girls.

Members of Interact clubs in London, England, stage a karate demonstration (top left) to raise funds . . . help out a disabled old-age pensioner by doing his yard work . . . and stage a marathon walk to raise money for charity . . . In San Luis Potosí, México (opposite page), Interact club members tutor boys in a reform school.

Corps in Africa wrote of a village's need for funds to complete a school, we responded by raising $400. Hospitality for overseas visitors and correspondence with them have proved to be popular international projects.

When five or more Interact clubs exist within a Rotary district, an Interact district may be formed and a district representative elected by the clubs. He encourages a flow of ideas among clubs, friendly competition on projects, mutual problem-solving, and group effort on projects of a larger scope.

When I worked with the different clubs in the district, I was struck by the basic similarities yet very individual characteristics of each club. No two clubs are alike. The spirit of each club depends upon its individuals—the youth, the advisors, the Rotarians. Yet, everywhere, to be a member of Interact is to strive with people of different backgrounds and different ages toward common goals—service to others and better world understanding.   —*Lisa Bollen*

Rotaract—partner in service

There is nothing quite like Rotaract. Born of Rotary and now a partner with Rotary, Rotaract has as its essence a certain idealism that only the young can know.

I first heard of Rotaract in 1969, when my employer, a Rotarian, invited me to an interest meeting called to form the Rotaract Club of Brisbane. At that time the only other Rotaract club in Australia and one of the few in the world was Brisbane West, chartered the year before. As I write this, there are some 35,000 young men and women aged 18 to 28 in some sixty countries who proudly wear the red and gold Rotaract badge. And I have spent five tremendous years of service with my fellow Rotaractors.

Most Rotaract clubs are made up of twenty to thirty young people—often with conflicting political, moral and religious views—actively working on their selected projects in community, international and vocational service towards one goal: a new world in which every person will be free of the chains of poverty, ill health, unhappiness, loneliness, and prejudice. Inevitably there are differences in opinion on how to reach this goal. But I can assure you—and the hundreds of successful projects and activities on every continent will bear me out—that Rotaract is a success.

Our first major community service project in Brisbane was the provision of a mobile kindergarten for use in some of the poorer areas of the city. The great pride we took in that success rapidly abated, however, with the realization that there is so much more that needs to be done in many areas.

Establishment of a library in Papua New Guinea, the gift of an auto engine for instruction in a city vocational school, food and clothing given to African famine victims, help for pensioners unable to maintain their own houses—such are the good things that have come about because of Rotaract and its interest.

Fund raising was often a game, great fun, rather than the painful exercise that many older groups seem to think it. Balls, cabarets, fairs and roadside stalls, bike-a-thons, squash-a-thons, raft-a-thons, anything-a-thons—you name it, and Rotaract has done it.

Many Rotaract projects involve time or talent or hard work rather than money. Thus, the Rotaract Club of Brisbane North each month hosts a group of some sixty old-age citizens on an excursion to the beach, a picnic in the park, or a concert; the program has been of tremendous value and enjoyment to both groups.

Over and over again I have seen the Rotaract badge become a passport to lasting friendship with young people of many nationalities. In 1971, I went to Saigon to present to a young orphan an educational assistance gift from the twenty-two Australian and Papua New Guinea Rotaract clubs of District 260. On the way I visited clubs in many southeast Asian nations, and found that the internationality of Rotary has truly found its way into Rotaract.

74

Organizational techniques that will last a lifetime are absorbed by Rotaractors at their weekly and fortnightly meetings. With the help of Rotarian counselors, they learn about club finance, public speaking, even catering. Guest speakers plant in their minds the seeds of new ideas and new perspectives from which will come the projects of the future.

John Gardner, a former U.S.A. cabinet member, has said:

The young people of this generation are perhaps more alert to the problems of the larger society than any preceding generation has been. But as they move into their careers it is all too likely that their concern will diminish. For all their activism, they show every indication of following the time-honored trend: a few years of indignant concern for social betterment, characterized by a demand for immediate solutions to all the world's problems, and then trailing off into the apathy and disinterest of the young executive or professional.

I for one do not think that those in the ranks of Rotaract will share such a fate. While each Rotaract member has joined for somewhat different reasons—some to meet new friends, to attain a fuller social life, to overcome loneliness and a feeling of alienation—all participate in work for the benefit of others. Rotaract enables young people to do more than complain and criticize—it gives them the green light to take action for the things that they want to see happen in the world.   —*Robert F. Whiddon*

Environmental projects are popular with Rotaract, a Rotary-sponsored service club for young adults. Here, in Port of Spain, Trinidad and Tobago, Rotaract joined with Rotary and 300 schoolchildren in cleaning up Queen's Park.

Rotaractors of Hornsby, Australia, held a raft race (top) to raise funds for a project . . . In Cochin, India, a housekeeping contest enrolled 175 participants; each house was inspected daily for a month . . . Rotaract club members of Kitami, Japan (opposite page), staged a winter program for handicapped children.

Friend to youth

Interest in the welfare of young people began in the early days of Rotary. For example, a popular early activity was sponsorship of Boys and Girls Week, a series of events to focus attention upon youngsters and their general welfare. Rotary club efforts led to the formation in the U.S.A. of the National Easter Seal Society for Crippled Children and Adults, and similar organizations in many other countries. Today Rotary clubs and individual Rotarians are engaged in a tremendous variety of youth service projects, as the photos on these pages testify. Each club chooses its own. Many clubs sponsor service clubs for young men and women. Called Interact and Rotaract, both organizations have goals similar to those of Rotary. They are like many other Rotary youth activities in that they build good citizenship by emphasizing service to the community, the nation, and the world.

Popular throughout Australia and New Zealand are Rotary Youth Leadership Award seminars for outstanding young people ages 17 to 24.

Youngsters of Plymouth, Michigan, U.S.A., learn about animals firsthand by visiting the "Rotary club school farm."

Sixteen schoolchildren (top) of Godthaab, Greenland, prepare to leave their
"foster parents" of Skanderborg, Denmark, after a three-months' stay
arranged by the Rotary club . . . In Minamata, Japan, safety flags help
schoolchildren cross streets . . . Kendo (opposite page) is one of the Rotary-
sponsored activities at a city recreation center for working youths in
Kuwana, Japan.

Handicapped boys and girls (top) practice their dexterity in the
Handi-Ham room of the Rotary Activities building at Camp Courage,
Maple Lake, Minnesota, U.S.A. . . . An open-air skittle alley was a gift
by the Rotary Club of Berlin, Federal Republic of Germany, to a special
home for youngsters receiving psychiatric treatment . . . At the Kitchener-
Waterloo Rotary Children's Centre (opposite page) some 525 handicapped
children undergo treatment. Rotarians of Kitchener and Waterloo, Ontario,
Canada, have helped the centre for more than fifty years and have raised
over a million dollars for it.

Children clamber over a Rotary elephant in a Porbandar, India, children's park . . . "Carols by candlelight" (opposite page) is a Christmas event sponsored by the Rotary Club of Goulburn-Mulwaree, Australia, and other service clubs.

Rotary and the world of work

Automation, ecology, recycling, job satisfaction, consumer relations, truth in advertising, urban stress, labor relations . . .

These are among the modern concerns of Rotarians who seek to serve through their vocations. "Vocational Service," as it is termed, has been an integral part of Rotary from its very beginning.

Men become members of a Rotary club by virtue of the jobs they hold. Each is chosen to represent his particular business or professional activity in his community, and this vocational variety gives Rotary its special stance and strength. When Paul P. Harris first conceived his idea for a service club he had more in mind than simply establishing a club for young lawyers like himself, or for businessmen. In forming a group of men from different businesses and professions, he sought to reconstruct in a large city the "mutual cooperation and informal friendship such as all of us had once known in our villages." There, storekeepers, doctors, attorneys, bankers, and others practiced their vocations in one small area of town. Because of this proximity, friendships sprang up easily and each man gained some practical knowledge of each other's business or profession.

The first Rotarians, wrote Paul Harris in his book, *My Road to Rotary*, helped each other vocationally "in every way that kindly heart and friendly spirit could suggest. . . . They patronized each other when it was practical to do so, exerted helpful influence and gave wise counsel when needed. Some realized business advantages, others did not. All realized the advantages of fellowship."

Opposite page: Young men are trained in valuable vocational skills at the hobby center sponsored by the Rotary Club of Jamshedpur, India.

For a time members were even provided with return postcards on which they reported weekly to the club statistician—a club officer—the number of business items they had received from other members and the orders, contracts, or patronage they had influenced or given outright themselves to their fellow Rotarians.

While this early form of vocational service undoubtedly attracted many businessmen to Rotary, Rotary could not have developed to its present-day form or even survived had not a new, important element been included, one that enabled Rotary to transcend the simple goals of increased friendship and personal profit. This third incentive was explained in *Rotary?*, a book-length report of a study made in 1934 by the Social Science Committee of the University of Chicago:

The conditions prevalent in the business community of Chicago in the early 1900s, and generally prevalent, in greater or lesser degree, throughout the western world since the industrial revolution, were not only productive of personal isolation, with a resulting starvation of social instincts of businessmen, they were likewise conducive to sharp and unscrupulous business practices, to chicanery and dishonesty, to an unrestricted and unprincipled pursuit of profit, to civic indifference, and to political corruption. . . . Any movement or organization which offered hope of civic regeneration, which held out opportunities for service, which was devoted to higher ideals of business practice and of political behavior, inevitably made a powerful appeal to those business and professional leaders who were sufficiently social-minded to be discontented with prevailing conditions. Here was a third incentive which drew to the movement some people who might have remained unmoved by opportunities for fellowship and profit. . . . Here was an incentive which tended progressively to crowd the profit motive into the background and to become the guiding light of the whole movement and which saved the club from the disintegration with which it was threatened in its earliest years.

In effect, the development of vocational service gave Rotary the survival ability which any mere association of businessmen, without a purpose, was bound to lack.

Credit for articulating the ideal usually goes to Arthur Frederick Sheldon, who in 1910 chaired the first committee on business methods of the original association of Rotary clubs. Sheldon was the founder of a school for salesmen based on the idea that successful salesmanship depends upon rendering service and that no transaction was justified unless both parties to a sale benefited. This idea he infused into the philosophy of Rotary.

Today vocational service is one of the four principal avenues of Rotary service (the others being club, community, and international service). Part of the object of Rotary as declared in every club constitution is "to encourage and foster high ethical standards in business and professions; the recognition of the worthiness of all useful occupations; and the dignifying by each Rotarian of his occupation as an opportunity to serve society."

88

Rotary exchange student Shelley K. Gane, of Howick, New Zealand, gets a glimpse of beef production on the Springville, Utah, U.S.A., farm of Rotarian Bill Averett.

Cartoons from a Rotary filmstrip make important points about vocational service: that each Rotarian represents a different vocation; that fairness to customers, recognition of all useful occupations for their service to society, fair benefits for employees, helping young people learn about opportunities in various careers, and enlightening fellow Rotarians about one's occupation are all a part of vocational service.

90

Vocational service stresses the need of each member to practice vocational service on a personal basis. It is held that the man who accepts the privilege of a classification in Rotary also undertakes a personal obligation. He is obliged to represent his own business or profession to his fellow Rotarians, and, at the same time, to represent the ideals of Rotary to his business or professional associates, employees, and colleagues.

Thus, during the early years of Rotary, Rotarians were urged by a convention resolution to compose right principles of conduct for their respective trades or professions. During the twelve years following, Rotarians were responsible for the adoption of codes of correct practice by 134 trade associations.

A popular way for Rotarians to inform each other about their respective vocations is the "my job" talk. This may be a five- or ten-minute segment of a weekly meeting, or it may occupy the entire program period. In some clubs, each new member, on the day he is inducted, speaks briefly about his work. In others, every member gives such a talk at successive meetings until all have spoken.

A popular vocational service project of Rotary clubs is promulgation of The Four-Way Test—a series of four questions about "the things we think, say, or do." The Test was formulated during the 1930s by Chicago Rotarian Herbert J. Taylor soon after he was made president of a nearly bankrupt kitchenware company. He conceived it as a way to develop in his company qualities which competitors would not have in equal amount —character, dependability, a willingness to serve. It seemed to work; the company prospered. Eventually Rotarian Taylor became president of Rotary International and transferred all rights in the Test to the organization. Its text:

THE FOUR-WAY TEST
of the things we think, say, or do
1. Is it the TRUTH?
2. Is it FAIR to all concerned?
3. Will it build GOODWILL and BETTER FRIENDSHIPS?
4. Will it be BENEFICIAL to all concerned?
© Rotary International

Many Rotarians keep copies of the Test in their places of business. Clubs sponsor essay contests on the Test in local schools. Some make it a community project, using billboards, newspaper and broadcast advertising and other promotions.

Reflecting their interest in young people, Rotarians provide advice on careers to students about to graduate from secondary schools. Some Rotary clubs furnish schools with lists of Rotarians willing to give individual counsel about their own businesses and professions. Other clubs or Rotary districts conduct career programs to which students and their parents are invited. Many Rotarians invite interested students to spend a day or more in their offices or factories to get the feel of the business world.

"Rotation Days" in Rotary clubs recapture the flavor of the earliest Rotary meetings, when members met at each other's places of business. After a regular meeting, the club is invited to visit or tour the workplace of a member.

One good way for Rotarians to propagate the ideal of Rotary in their vocations is through their employees. The Rotary Club of London, England, once polled its 200 members and discovered that collectively they employed more than 250,000 people.

Some clubs hold special Rotary meetings to which members are asked to bring an employee. A club may present an award to an employee or to someone such as a doctor, nurse, teacher or policeman who has served the community with distinction through his vocation. Or a club may stage a community-wide courtesy contest with a prize for the most courteous public-contact employee.

In the early days of Rotary, when vocational service was known as "business methods," a member with a business problem might bring it up at a meeting and ask for advice. This idea today has been formalized in various programs. One, usually a one-day event, is known as a business-relations conference. Experts on various aspects of business talk about and answer questions on new business developments and techniques, accounting methods, employee morale, and standards of business conduct and ethics. In a further development of this idea, "small business clinics" are conducted, with emphasis on help-ing potential owners of small business, especially members of disadvantaged groups who have had little or no business experience.

Their annual international convention provides Rotarians with an opportunity to enjoy a rare vocational service experience—that of meeting Rotarians from all over the world who share the same or a related vocational classification. A feature of Rotary conventions for decades has been an afternoon devoted to vocational craft assemblies. In one of fifty-five simultaneous meetings, Rotarians discuss with their vocational counter-parts various topics relating to the theme of the convention or to vocational service aims.

All of these activities reflect the seriousness with which Rotarians regard vocational service, which can be thought of as the seed from which sprang Rotary's ideal of service to mankind.

To a large extent, the public is unaware of this side of Rotary. It associates Rotary with its more overt works in the community, such as aiding the handicapped, senior citizens outings, or establishing a city park. But vocational service is no less worthy, for it deals with one of the most fundamental aspects of life.

Work is what man must do to survive, as an individual and as a community. By his occupation a man defines himself: "I am an attorney, a physician, a carpenter. . . ." And although the ancients often referred to work as a curse and a punishment of the gods, work gives aim and purpose to the lives of men. Even in their leisure men turn to acti-vities such as fishing and hunting and hobbies that may involve greater physical effort than they exert "at work."

One of the most serious challenges to be faced in modern vocational service is that, for many, work has lost its meaning. Amid the routine of the assembly line, the joy of craftsmanship has vanished. Overshadowed by the increasing complexities of mass production and mass marketing, one's contribution seems less and less important.

In this atmosphere, Rotary's challenge is to find new ways to further "the recognition of the worthiness of all useful occupations; and the dignifying by each Rotarian of his occupation as an opportunity to serve society."

One portent of the future comes from Sweden, where an automobile manufacturer has transformed his method of building cars from a series of repetitive, dulling movements on an assembly line to one in which teams of workers build entire cars, one by one, like craftsmen rather than robots.

A Japanese firm founded by a Rotarian continues a program of enriching employees' hours in the factory with exercise breaks, music, philosophy, and extracurricular activities.

In Germany, workers achieve a greater sense of participation and responsibility in their work through representation on their companies' boards of directors.

"High ethical standards in business and professions" is still another vocational service phrase with broad application to current concerns. The just employer provides equal pay and opportunities in response to equal performance—whether by male or female, young or old, or member of a minority group. The ethical manufacturer considers the impact of his plant upon the quality of life in his community, upon air and water and natural resources. The fair-dealing retailer accepts the return of merchandise that doesn't live up to his promises, stated or implied.

The ideals of vocational service are woven into the very fabric of the Rotarian's business and professional life, inseparable, yet not easy to define. "Vocational service," in the words of one Rotarian, "is putting Rotary to work where we work—and in all our lives."   —*Albert N. Stephanides*

Serving society through the job

Rotary club membership is based on vocations. A Rotary club attempts to have a representative of each business or profession in the community which it serves. Membership in a Rotary club obligates the man to seek ways better to serve society through the vocation he represents. This concept is called "vocational service." Some of the visible manifestations of vocational service are work with youth in the form of career conferences, efforts to improve standards of practices and products through professional and trade association work, and addresses or activities designed to give others an insight into one's specific business or profession.

Scores of blind persons have been trained and placed in industry in a project of the Rotary Club of São Paulo-Itaim, Brazil.

A good job (top left) in a Rotarian's warehouse for this young man resulted from a training and placement program run by the Rotary Clubs of Toronto and East York, Ontario, Canada . . . In a Turkish village (top right), training in the art of rugmaking is assisted by the Rotary Club of Cankaya . . . Baking (bottom left) is one of many trades taught at the Vocational Technical Institute in Guatemala, launched with the help of Guatemala City Rotarians . . . Girls learn tailoring at the vocational craft center run by the Rotary Club of Madras, India.

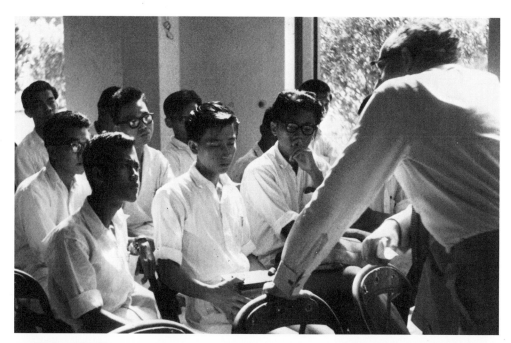

In Singapore (top), some 500 students of twenty-eight schools attend a careers conference sponsored by a Rotary club . . . In Lyon, France, a Rotarian manager of an advertising agency tells students about his work. They are among 2,500 attending "Operation Career" sponsored by six area Rotary clubs . . . The Four-Way Test (opposite page), here presented to a college, is used around the world.

PRESENTED TO
PEPPERDINE COLLEGE AT MALIBU
BY THE
SANTA MONICA ROTARY CLUB

THE FOUR-WAY TEST
OF THE THINGS WE THINK, SAY OR DO:

1. IS IT THE TRUTH?
2. IS IT FAIR TO ALL CONCERNED?
3. WILL IT BUILD GOOD WILL AND BETTER FRIENDSHIPS?
4. WILL IT BE BENEFICIAL TO ALL CONCERNED?

International friendship
in action

I happened at a fireside meeting. The topic was "What Rotary Is—to Me." A leathery-faced outdoorsman was speaking. He had been a Rotarian for twenty years—one of our community leaders.

"To me," he began, "Rotary means *international*—international friendship." His intent blue gaze swept the dozen attentive faces around the room. Continuing—"You're surprised to hear me say that, aren't you? I've been a narrow sort of person much of my life. I've never had much concern for peoples outside my country; in fact, I've been a little antagonistic. But Rotary has changed me. I admit it. I'm proud of it."

My friend had been active in a host of civic and service organizations—two or three of them international in scope—and we would never have called him provincial. But it was impressive to me, a fairly new member of our Rotary club, to hear him attribute to his Rotary club associations a significant change in his attitude toward international affairs. Later, I came to understand why.

It is Rotary *International*, the worldwide organization to which Rotary clubs belong. It became international in 1910 with the founding of the Rotary Club of Winnipeg, Canada, and crossed the Atlantic in 1911 when the Rotary Club of Dublin, Ireland, was established. From those pioneering days Rotary clubs have been organized in every part of the world where citizens are free to group themselves in voluntary association. In particular they have been especially summoned by the fourth aspect of Rotary's object:

Opposite page: The annual convention of Rotary International draws some 15,000 Rotarians and their families from around the world. Here, at the Atlanta convention, a little girl and a Rotarian from the U.S.A. make friends with a Rotarian from Jamaica.

"The advancement of international understanding, goodwill, and peace. . . ."

Rotary International, as an association, has an indispensable role in the process of linking Rotarian to Rotarian, club to club, and district to district. The messages are continuous and variegated. They flow in all the languages of Rotary. They are as uncomplicated as a simple letter from a Rotarian in Argentina to his counterpart in New Zealand and as complex as the Rotarians of Lisieux, France, initiating a district-wide program for providing nutritional supplements to Burundi, in Africa, to help fight the deficiency disease kwashiorkor.

International movements, bodies, and organizations today number into the thousands—most with worthy goals and activities. But Rotary International stands tall in breadth and scope of membership and in its influence for goodwill and peace. With more countries represented in its membership than in the United Nations, it embraces all creeds, colors, and nationalities. It pleads no special cause or ideology, welcoming all men who can assemble freely and work together without external interference. It has no secrets, impinges upon no other group, and exalts no personal heroes. It stresses each individual's involvement in efforts to promote world peace.

A president of Rotary International has spoken to the point of personal participation: "The fact that the water of an ocean doesn't lap on your doorstep doesn't mean you are barred from international service. You can always write a letter to another Rotary club to establish communication . . . it is the individual response which is basic to Rotary and that response brings its own reward."

Something as simple as the exchange of a slide program for a showing at a Rotary club meeting can be the springboard for cooperation between participating clubs in a World Community Service Project. World community service is a logical extension of local community service, the "global village" concept—that one community's problems are another's even though an ocean or a continent or both may separate the two. Contacts between Rotarians help match clubs which need help with clubs which can give help.

One notable example of successful world community service involves an orphanage on Koje Island off the southern coast of Korea. There a woman struggled to care for her charges. The children drank from a distant well, washed their clothes in a brook, and used grimy oil lamps—there was no electric power.

The Rotary Club of Pusan South undertook to tell her story and to administer whatever aid came in. Hearing the story, Rotarians of Lansing, Michigan, U.S.A., sent $3,000; and $1,500 came from other Rotarians in District 636, Michigan.

Another such project has been carried on by Rotary clubs in Germany and Austria cooperating with Rotary clubs in Peru to help build a school in Chincha, Peru; more than $26,000 has been contributed.

It isn't always money that's needed most; sometimes it's people who can share business

100

or professional expertise. A Mexico City Rotarian took his skills to Guayaquil, Ecuador, and stayed a month counseling local businessmen and small factory managers. A Hershey, Pennsylvania, U.S.A., Rotarian journeyed to Pakistan to do the same thing. Numerous Rotarians from Japan have shared their professional skills in India.

In a world shrunken in space and time Rotarians have wider and better opportunities than any other international group to explore ways of developing a more peaceful world, without condescension or fear, and to apply their hands-outstretched techniques.

Those hands are multiplied a thousandfold by the young persons sponsored by Rotarians in dozens of diverse projects. Most notable of these efforts is The Rotary Foundation, conceived in 1917. It was given dramatic, worldwide impetus in 1947 when, as a memorial to Rotary's founder, Paul Harris, a program for graduate study was launched. The Rotary Foundation has expanded to include Undergraduate Fellowships, Technical Training, Teachers of the Handicapped, Group Study Exchange, and Special Grants. In a recent year there were more than 800 recipients of educational awards, representing sixty-five countries; they studied in forty-nine host countries. There were 465 Group Study Exchange team members representing twenty-four countries and hosted in twenty-six countries. All these young men and women serve as "ambassadors of goodwill" in addition to pursuing their studies. They enjoy thousands of people-to-people contacts during their year, and on return they share their insights with people of their home countries. Contributions to the Foundation permit the distribution of more than 5 million dollars a year in awards.

Impressive though these expenditures are, they are not just money. These kinds of funds invested in tomorrow's leaders translate into illuminating and meaningful acts of helpfulness, lowering the level of ideological misunderstanding.

Typical of The Rotary Foundation's Special Grant activity is a $2,000 award to District 265, New South Wales, Australia, to assist in the completion of Dauli Teacher's College, Papua New Guinea. Combining Foundation and district funds, plus their own labor and the resources of an interdenominational church group, Rotarians have helped construct forty buildings for the college, including dormitories for 400 trainee teachers.

Olivier Reverdin, president of the Swiss Council of Science, told Rotary's international convention in Lausanne, Switzerland, that "the true way to work for peace . . . is to weave around the world a tight web of personal relationships so that stereotypes, which historically have aroused hatred among people and incited them to war, will forever disappear." The "web" is strengthened even more by club and district youth exchange projects which have burgeoned in recent years. In a recent year, some 5,400 young persons spent time abroad under such sponsorship; more than 2,400 students spent a full school year abroad, living in homes—generally Rotarians'—in their host community.

The simple lines of Rotary communications are equally adaptable to disaster. Hardly a major disaster comes to pass without the humanitarian concern of Rotarians coming to a focus on the troubled spot.

Most aid, of course, flows through relief agencies, but on some occasions it is sent direct. When, for example, an earthquake devastated Managua, Nicaragua, the Rotary Club of Guatemala Sur, Guatemala, flew a quantity of the most urgently needed medicines to Managua within two days. It also organized a "Rotary Bread to Managua" drive, providing 4,000 to 8,000 loaves daily. With Rotary Clubs of Masaya and Granada, Nicaragua, the Guatemala Sur Rotarians joined to build a bread factory in Granada to provide 36,000 loaves daily. Other Rotary clubs rushed to provide help in numerous forms, all channeled through Rotarians without red tape or bureaucracy.

The individual Rotarian is the key to the success of all international service. He tells himself: "Let peace begin with me." And it does.

This process is threaded throughout Rotary discussions and literature and highlighted every September during World Understanding Week. Probably half the Rotary clubs in the world employ the week to put the spotlight on their internationality. They have international guests, sponsor international festivals, debate policies in international contention, and examine their own international projects.

The Rotarian magazine and its Spanish-language edition, *Revista Rotaria*, provide background information for many stimulating discussions during this week. These publications, as well as all the others, deal forthrightly with controversial subjects absorbing the minds of all Rotarians in times of intense social change. Topics include world government, nuclear disarmament, the United Nations, the Common Market, population problems, the human environment, activist youth, and many others equally provocative.

In a similar spirit of "search and understand" the annual international convention probes fundamental issues. Themes such as "A New Look at World Peace" characterize these meetings. Fellowship is the great amalgam blending more than 15,000 persons from one hundred countries. It is a great international idea exchange.

An appropriate metaphor in the Space Age refers to our planet as "Spaceship Earth," and it was used by U.S. Astronaut Edgar D. Mitchell at the recent convention in Lausanne, Switzerland. The sixth man to set foot on the moon painted a vivid picture of earth as viewed from outer space. He asked the contentious planet a question: "How long can man fail to see that all life is but the crew of a small planetary spaceship, a crew that must work in harmony, conserve its resources, and function as a team if that spaceship is to survive?"

He answered his question with a principle: "The ultimate survival of a culture is dependent upon the survival of all cultures. The parochial differences must be set aside."

That's what our fellow Rotarian at the fireside meeting was saying to us that night. Rotary had helped him set aside those differences.   —*Harvey C. Jacobs*

The Rotary Foundation: education for peace

Through The Rotary Foundation, Rotary International is among the leading sponsors of overseas study by young adults. The program is different from almost all others in that each student serves as an ambassador of goodwill between the host and home countries. Awardees report that this special dimension of their program is envied by other international students, many of whom have few contacts with people of their country of study.

Members of Rotary clubs and members of their families are not eligible for Rotary Foundation awards, which include grants worth more than five million dollars a year to men and women for a year of study abroad—graduates and undergraduates, technical trainees (like Soloman Abe, of Nigeria [below], studying textile design in the U.S.A.), teachers of the handicapped—and to five-man group study exchange teams of young business and professional men who tour another country for four to eight weeks as guests of Rotarians and Rotary clubs.

Paul Carter (hand raised), a Rotary Foundation technical trainee from England, directs a movie as part of his overseas study at a U.S. photography institute . . . Francine Kamen (opposite page) shows Edward Wendt and James Jones the location of the University of Tucumán in Argentina, where she studied as a Rotary Foundation graduate fellow. Both men are directors of the Rotary Club of Hightstown-South Brunswick, New Jersey, U.S.A., which nominated her.

A Group Study Exchange Team from North Carolina, U.S.A., visits a ship works in Barrow-in-Furness, England, during their two-month study tour as guests of English Rotary clubs . . . Chicago's 102-story John Hancock building (opposite page) is one of the memories a study team from Japan will take home.

A Group Study Exchange Team from southern Japan—five young men and their group leader—visit for several weeks in northwest Illinois, U.S.A., as guests of Rotary clubs. They tour a clutch plant (bottom), one of many factories on their itinerary; a park where a famous American Indian statue overlooks the Rock River; and are warmly welcomed (opposite page), lodged, and cared for in the homes of Rotarians. The following year, a Group Study Exchange Team from this area will be guests of Rotary clubs in the district that sponsored this team.

Youth exchange across the borders

A guest for a year in a German school and German homes, Australian Sue Sutton (opposite page) is part of one of the great success stories of Rotary. Each year more than 5,000 young people like Sue are exchanged across international borders under the auspices of individual Rotary clubs. She is pictured presenting the banner of the Rotary club in her home city of Kiama, Australia, to the president of her host Rotary club in Bad Berleburg, Germany; as a guest in a Rotary home; playing in the snow with a Rotary family's children; museum peeking; helping out in the kitchen—for during her year she is treated just like a member of the family or families with whom she stays; and with classmates of the high school in Bad Berleburg. At first, she had trouble speaking German but gradually became adept at conversation and even slang, made many friends in school, and became so at home with her host family that she refers to them as "Mutti" (Mother) and "Vati" (Father). As a result of her stay in Germany, says her father, "Sue has a broadened outlook, more interest in world news, a greater maturity . . . and much more confidence in coping with new situations. Sue sums it up as 'a great year.'"

Youth exchange, primarily of pre-university students 16 to 18 years of age, works very simply. A club in one country makes arrangements with a club in another country to host a young person from its community. While abroad, the youngster in effect is "adopted" by the entire Rotary club and lives as a member of one or more host families while attending the local high school. School administrators welcome these students and usually waive tuition, for their presence helps to broaden the perspectives of all students with whom they come into contact. In Europe, a popular form of student exchange is a "three-week round trip" which provides for visits to interesting sites and living in Rotarians' homes.

Japan is a favorite country of Western Youth exchange students, which may be guessed from these scenes: of Australian Glenda Jackson (top) enjoying a beach outing with Rotaract members of Noogata, Japan; of students donning "happi coats" as part of a warm welcome from Rotarians of Komagane, Japan; of Marianne McArthur (opposite page) in a ceremonial photo arranged by Rotarian hosts of Yanagawa, Japan, to send back home to St. George, Utah, U.S.A.

Global neighbors

The project may be a new well for an impoverished rural
village, books for a school which has none, or medical supplies
for a jungle medical clinic. World community service is a
significant Rotary program in which a Rotary club or district
in one country sends aid to a Rotary club service effort in
another country. The object is to accomplish a needed project
that will help raise the standard of living and increase understanding between the two communities. The local club in-
vestigates and reports on the problem; a club abroad hears
about it and provides aid which the local club administers
(and frequently adds to). Although in most cases the project is
small in terms of the immense needs of an underdeveloped
country, it may get a promising venture started. The process
of providing help calls attention to the need; it helps to create
better-informed attitudes among Rotarians and the public in
both countries. And these attitudes may influence government
and others to support the more massive undertakings necessary
to improve the quality of life in the problem area.

Seventy-eight cartons of books for Fiji schoolchildren, collected in a drive by Rotarians of Cairns, Australia, are swung aboard ship . . . U.S.A. Rotarian Everett Rolff (opposite page) reads to youngsters in the new children's library of Patzcuaro, México; he organized a drive that resulted in donation to the library of $10,000 by northern California (U.S.A.) Rotary clubs.

World Understanding Week (top) is globally observed in Rotary; in Margao, India, it prompted an international understanding exhibition . . . Breeding better rice is among the activities of the Philippine Rural Reconstruction Movement, which has attracted funds from Rotary clubs abroad . . . This village well in India (opposite page) was financed by Rotary clubs in the Federal Republic of Germany.

117

In Papua New Guinea, medical missionary Dorothy Elphick (white dress) exchanges the grass hut (top) in which she had worked for fourteen years for a new medical building, a gift of the Rotary Club of Brisbane West, Australia . . . Donated eyeglasses (opposite page) are collected by Toledo, Ohio, Rotarians for the needy in India.

119

A friend of children in Kathmandu, Nepal, is Dr. N. Iwamura, whose community health work is backed by churches and by Rotarians in Japan . . . Medical supplies and instruments (opposite page) were given by the Rotary Club of Pleasant Hills, Pennsylvania, U.S.A., to start a mobile clinic in Papua New Guinea.

What Rotary means to the individual

Amazing," thought the psychiatrist as he stepped from a taxi in downtown Sydney, Australia. "The taxi driver talked to me! What a wonderful country this is."

The psychiatrist, a Japanese Rotarian who had just arrived in Sydney to attend a Rotary International convention, had been greeted by the driver as he got into the taxi at the airport: "Very nice day, isn't it?" The two men had talked enjoyably until the end of the ride.

In his home country, mused the psychiatrist, a pleasant conversation between a taxi driver and his passenger seldom if ever happened. Especially in Tokyo, a taxi driver would take you where you wanted to go without uttering a single word.

But about a half century ago, recalled the traveler, when he was a young boy, taxi drivers were not so unfriendly. Then, the population of Tokyo, now the world's largest city, was only one-tenth of today's figure. Perhaps the change in the drivers' attitude was related to the increase in population.

That's it, he thought; look at Australia: her land area is twenty times that of Japan, but her population is only about one-tenth as large. Australia's neighbor, New Zealand, is about the same size as Japan but has only one-fiftieth as many people. In these two neighboring countries, many beautiful spots remain in their original natural state; the air and water are still clean. And at the same time, the people who live in these countries obviously are kind and thoughtful.

Opposite page: Friendships grow in the congenial atmosphere of the club, as here in Bahía Blanca, Argentina.

123

Somehow, thought the psychiatrist, when the population increases, the danger of air and water pollution increases—and also the danger of mental pollution in men.

Similar phenomena in other areas could be cited. For example, once a tranquil spa located deep in the mountains or on a beautifully isolated island becomes famous as a tourist resort, the kindness and warmheartedness of the local people rapidly changes and is coarsened by the crowds of tourists. It is conceivable that when Chicago was merely a small village, its people were unspoiled and kind, and enjoyed affectionate friendships.

But when Paul Harris, the founder of Rotary, came to live there in 1896, it seemed to him that the people were unfriendly, as compared with residents of the smaller towns of his boyhood, and that Chicago was a lonely place.

One might imagine, thought the psychiatrist, that the people of Australia and New Zealand are a kindly, special breed, different from those of other lands. But he knew this was not so. Comparative psychological studies of the peoples of the world have revealed that the distribution of temperament and the ratio of mental disorders is much the same from one country to another.

But why is it that only in less-populated areas such as Australia do most of the people one meets seem to be of a warm and thoughtful disposition? Why, when the population increases, does a mental pollution seem to occur?

Perhaps, reasoned the psychiatrist, the causes are these: Among all people there is a small percentage who have abnormal personalities either because of heredity or the influence of others. Their actions frequently disappoint or shock normal, warmhearted people. If we deal only with small numbers of people, and with people we already know, as in a small town, we do not often meet these ill ones. But the more people we become involved with, as in a large city, the more often we are likely to encounter people exhibiting abnormal behaviors. This is the mechanism that causes our own mental pollution: To protect ourselves we become defensive, less friendly, and more suspicious of the next stranger.

It is a sad but undeniable fact that our minds become polluted or distorted little by little as we meet and involve with many kinds of people in our efforts to make our living.

"Is there any remedy?" thought the psychiatrist.

Each person has his own solution, he told himself, and it appears that there are many different kinds of successful remedies. He knew of many people in his own land and elsewhere who had found ways to remain kind and thoughtful despite the stresses of urban living.

For him, he knew, and for thousands of other visitors to Sydney that day, there was an obvious remedy for mental pollution: Rotary. Rotary meetings, whether a weekly club meeting, a district conference, or an international convention, each helps to counteract mental pollution in members. And why? Because Rotarians are carefully selected persons of good character. When members attend Rotary meetings, they do not have to be defensive or cautious toward anyone present. They know from previous experience that whatever Rotary meeting they attend, in their own community or another, they will be surrounded by trustworthy, thoughtful men.

Even when he visits a Rotary club in a country where he cannot speak the language, the traveling Rotarian feels at home among the warm and understanding minds of everyone present. He communicates with others by gestures and facial expressions, and knows that "our hearts speak the same language."

So Rotary meetings act to cleanse the minds of members. As Paul Harris wrote—whenever he attended a Rotary meeting, he returned to his boyish mind.

However, the effect of Rotary is not limited to curing mental pollution. It has a more positive effect on the individual Rotarian. It changes his character so that he becomes more worthy and valuable to his community—and to himself. How does this happen?

There is a positive counterpart to the negative mental states we refer to as "complexes," which play a big role in the formation and development of our characters. A complex is a mix of feelings, memories, and impulses, caused by past experiences usually related to anger, frustration, or disappointment. Some of these memories are related to experiences so vividly recalled that one becomes angry each time one thinks of them; others are only subconsciously remembered, but still rankle. In any case, when we are angered or shamed or anguished by memories or undesirable experiences, our minds are frustrated and our characters tend little by little to become less desirable.

On the other hand, when we have many pleasant and inspirational experiences, by associating with people of warm understanding and kind hearts, how our minds and characters can change! Our personalities become more affirmative to life in general; we wish others to be happy and cheerful.

Rotarians improve their thinking and character when they participate personally in various Rotary activities. It is not enough simply to pay one's share of the club's expenses, as do many who tell themselves they have "no time" for gatherings and activities.

In almost every Rotary club in the world, there is at least one enthusiastic member who has been nicknamed "Mr. Rotary" or "Mr. Rotarian" by his fellows. In most cases, he was not an enthusiast from the start; what made him change and become enthusiastic was a certain inspirational experience he gained while engaged in a Rotary activity. Once he began to participate more fully in Rotary activities, he was exposed to more inspirational experiences, which further accelerated his enthusiasm.

Thus, the reward for striving to be a truly active Rotarian is a kinder heart and a finer character.

That is what a Japanese psychiatrist thought as he walked toward his hotel in Sydney, after he was greeted by the taxi driver: "Very nice day, isn't it?"   —*Hiroji Mukasa*

125

Fun and fellowship

In his own Rotary club, the typical Rotarian enjoys the kind of camaraderie which Rotary's founder Paul Harris sought when he formed in Chicago a small club of business and professional men, trying to recapture some of the friendliness and informality that characterized the small Vermont town where he was reared. Over the years, the one Rotary club became thousands, but the structure of Rotary remained simple: A man belongs to a Rotary club, which provides an opportunity for fellowship, a channel for his service efforts, and a weekly exposure to topics of community, national, or international interest. The Rotary world is divided into some 360 districts, each served voluntarily by a district governor who for a year visits clubs, organizes new clubs, and helps and instructs club officers and committeemen. Rotary clubs, in annual international conventions held in cities such as Montreal, Tokyo, Sydney, Paris, and Honolulu, elect a president and a board of directors of Rotary International, the association of Rotary clubs.

A Rotarian of Moorestown, New Jersey, U.S.A., shares a "bump" with an entertainer during a Rotary club Ladies' Night . . . At a meeting of the Rotary Club of Taipei South, Taiwan, Republic of China (opposite page), a member receives applause and a trophy.

Rotary upon occasion involves ceremony and royalty. The king and queen of Thailand (top) arrive at a Rotary art exhibition in Bangkok . . . Princess Benedikte of Denmark and Count Flemming of Rosenborg, then president of the Rotary Club of Copenhagen, at the club's 50th anniversary event.

Styles of charter nights range from rather formal, such as the launching of the Rotary Club of Hamble Valley, England, (top) to somewhat more relaxed, as in California, U.S.A., when Rotarians of San Rafael presented the new Rotary Club of Novato with its charter.

The central office of Rotary International (top) is in Evanston, Illinois, U.S.A. . . . Good fellowship abounds at a Rotary district conference, as here in Como, Italy, where the city's mayor (left) greets a past Rotary governor . . . Former president of Rotary International William C. Carter (opposite page) of England, chatting here with Rotarians of São Paulo, Brazil, traveled the globe during his term. As do all presidents of R.I., he served voluntarily for a full year, promoting Rotary's aims.

Meetings of all kinds: Rotarians of Can-Tho, Vietnam (top left), stage a world understanding party with members and guests from ten countries . . . For variety, the Rotary Club of Kalgoorlie, Australia, holds a meeting in a gold mine . . . The board of directors of the Rotary Club of Colombo, Sri Lanka, meets monthly to guide the club's course . . . The mayor of Houston, Texas, U.S.A. (opposite page), flanked by questioning reporters, discusses civic topics before his city's Rotary club, which, with more than 850 members, is the largest in the world.

Annually, each Rotary district holds an assembly to train incoming club officers, and a conference for information and inspiration open to all Rotarians in the district . . . In Alexandria, Arab Republic of Egypt (above), a district conference opens . . . Community singing (opposite page) adds spirit to a district assembly held in Makati, Philippines.

Rotary fellowship takes many forms, ranging from fireside meetings in homes, to a physical fitness log pull exercise (opposite page) by Rotarians of Zurich-Knonaueramt, Switzerland; an annual curling night in North Bay, Ontario, Canada; work projects (top) like the restoration of an old country water mill by the Rotary Club of Stord, Norway; and an exercise program for Rotarians of Halmstad, Sweden, to trim waistlines and protect hearts.

Rotary gatherings deliberately ignore regional and national boundaries and differences. A Rotary "Fly-In" (above) attracts 140 planes to Vacaville, California, U.S.A. Many of the pilots are members of the International Fellowship for Flying Rotarians, one of many avocational groups within Rotary including amateur radio operators, yachtsmen, and stamp collectors . . . At Dublin, Ireland (opposite page), members of three area clubs board a jet for a twenty-minute flight to lunch with Limerick Shannon Rotarians . . . In a historic mansion in Dusseldorf, Federal Republic of Germany, Rotarians and their wives host Rotary couples from Saint Nicholas-Waes, Belgium.

The Object of Rotary

The object of Rotary is to encourage and foster
the ideal of service as a basis of worthy enterprise
and, in particular, to encourage and foster:

First. The development of acquaintance as an
opportunity for service;

Second. High ethical standards in business and
professions; the recognition of the worthiness of
all useful occupations; and the dignifying by each
Rotarian of his occupation as an opportunity
to serve society;

Third. The application of the ideal of service
by every Rotarian to his personal, business and
community life;

Fourth. The advancement of international
understanding, goodwill and peace through a
world fellowship of business and professional
men united in the ideal of service.

Credits

The World of Rotary is published by Rotary International and was produced with the help of Rotarians worldwide by the secretariat of Rotary International, located in Evanston, Illinois, U.S.A.

Editor of the book is Elliott McCleary, a writer and editor of Evanston, Illinois. He is a former assistant editor of *The Rotarian*, official magazine of Rotary International.

Design consultant is Lawrence Levy, who heads a graphic design and filmmaking studio in Evanston.

The World of Rotary is available in five language editions: English, French, Japanese, Portuguese, and Spanish. It was translated from English into French by Julia Yardley; into Japanese by Zenji Furubayashi, Takaichi Miwa, Tsutomu Obana, Fumiko Oyamada and Teizo Shiohara Kane; into Portuguese by Alayde Cazão, and into Spanish by Alfonso Rubiano and Ramón Orellana.

Authors

Charles W. Ferguson, of Mt. Kisco, New York, U.S.A., is a former senior editor of *The Reader's Digest* and author of a book about service clubs, *Fifty Million Brothers*. J. P. Duminy, of Rondebosch, South Africa, has served Rotary International as first vice-president and the University of Cape Town as principal and vice-chancellor. Bhichai Rattakul is managing director of a pharmaceutical manufacturing firm in Bangkok, Thailand, a member of the Thailand Parliament, and serves on the Public Relations Committee of Rotary International. Rotarian Harold Hunt is emeritus professor of Classical Studies in the University of Melbourne, Australia, and the author of the book, *The Story of Rotary in Australia*. Alberto Pires Amarante is a past district governor of Rotary International, a consulting engineer of Rio de Janeiro, Brazil, and editor of the Rotary regional magazine, *Brasil Rotario*. Past First Vice-President of Rotary International Warren E. Kraft is an advertising executive of Seattle, Washington, U.S.A. Ernst G. Breitholtz, of Kalmar, Sweden, is a past president of Rotary International. John H. B. Savage is a retired area officer of the British Council in Southampton, England and has served Rotary International in Great Britain and Ireland as president. Tristano Bollelli is professor of linguistics at the University of Pisa, Italy, and is a past third vice-president of Rotary International. Andrew Robert Dreaver, a retired headmaster of Henderson, New Zealand, is a former member of the Youth Activities Committee of Rotary International. Robert F. Whiddon, of Canberra, is Secretary to the Minister for Aboriginal Affairs in the Australian parliament, and is a former district Rotaract representative in Australia. Former Interact Representative Lisa Bollen lives in Santa Barbara, California. Albert N. Stephanides, of Evanston, Illinois, U.S.A., is assistant editor specializing in vocational service in the program publications department of the secretariat of Rotary International. Harvey C. Jacobs, editor of the *Indianapolis News,* Indianapolis, Indiana, U.S.A., is a past district governor and former Under Secretary of Rotary International. Hiroji Mukasa is a psychiatrist in Nakatsu, Japan, and is a trustee of The Rotary Foundation.

Photographs

Rotary International gratefully acknowledges the efforts of Rotarians and Rotary clubs around the world who arranged for and contributed the photographs for this book. Many Rotary clubs did so as participants in the Rotary World Photo Contest, which drew more than 1,000 entries comprising 3,000 pictures. Several Rotary regional magazines provided pictures. In addition, credit is given for the photographs on the following pages: 10 Tom Bochsler / 23 (bottom) J. R. Mukherjee / 24 Holiday Fotos Ltd. / 31 Tradelinks Photo / 39 Dudley, Hardin & Yang, Inc. / 40 Hedrich-Blessing / 41 Peter Marcus / 44 André Gamet, S.A.R.L. /

46 Group Three Photography, Ltd. / 47 Richard Davis, L.R.P.S. / 53 (top) Ron Nielsen / 56 (bottom) Raettig Photo Service / 57 Ron Nielsen / 62 (top) Busselen Photographers; (bottom) The Natwar Art Studio / 65 (top left) Guzman; (top right) *The Natal Witness;* (lower left) Ron Nielsen; (lower right) L. & D. Keen Pty. Ltd. / 72 Michael Simpson / 73 Three Lions, Inc. / 75 Trinidad Express Newspapers, Ltd. / 76 (bottom) Tradelinks Photo / 78 Warringah Commercial Photography Pty. Ltd. / 79 Gaffield Studio / 82 (bottom) Titzenthaler-Foto / 84 The Natwar Art Studio / 90 cartoons by John Everds / 94 Foto Mumia / 95 (top left) Gilbert A. Milne & Co. Ltd.; (bottom left) Three Lions, Inc. / 97 City Center Photography / 98 Wayne Wilson / 104 Harold Rosenthal / 106 Barrow News & Mail / 107, 108, 109 Kaz Ayukawa / 111 Tony Griffin Kent / 115 John H. Desch Studio / 116 Studio Foto Lite / 117 (top) Raikar / 118 *Toledo Blade* / 119 L. & D. Keen Pty. Ltd. / 121 Ed. Walsh / 127 Ralph I. Shockey / 129 (bottom) Clif Rattenbury / 130 (top) Kranzten Studio Inc. / 135 Foto Center Philippines / 136 Hartmans Foto AB

A note on manufacture

The text and captions have been set in Linofilm Caledonia, the headings in Typositor Times Roman. Black and white pages were printed on Warren's Patina Matte, and the color pages on Mead Black and White. The cover material is Joanna Western Natural Finish Buckram. The book was printed and bound by R.R. Donnelley & Sons Company, Chicago, Illinois, U.S.A.